BELL'S EYE

Twenty Years of Drawing Blood

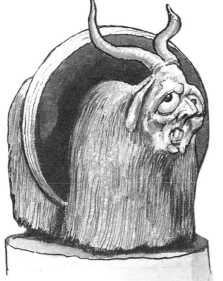

Acknowledgements

Thanks firstly to Brian Homer, without whom there wouldn't be any books; to Chris Kentish, Jim Deaves and William Bell for helping produce this one. I'm eternally grateful to my brother, Pete Bell and my old friend Paul Stevens for helping me develop the cartoon habit. I'd like to thank everybody who's ever given me work over the years, including Hunt Emerson at the erstwhile Birmingham Arts Lab Press; the late, great Ian Walker at the *Leveller*; Duncan Campbell at *Time Out/City Limits*; Mike McNay, Peter Preston and Alan Rusbridger at *The Guardian*, not forgetting Les Gibbard who so graciously let me steal his job; Tim Gopsill at the *Journalist*; Stuart Weir at the *New Statesman*; Geoffrey Strachan, Michael Earley and Eleanor Knight at Methuen Publishing and Bob Godfrey and all at Bob Godfrey Films. Thanks are also due to Michael White, Simon Hoggart and all on the political wing of *The Guardian* for their hospitality during the party conference season. I'd especially like to thank Kipper Williams firstly for loaning me back the artwork on page 73, but also for showing it was possible to make a living as a cartoonist back when we were both students in Leeds. I'd also like to thank him and David Austin for letting me hang around their studio for so many years. More thanks than I could ever express and enormous hugs to Will, Joe, Pad, Kit Kat and Heather for making it all worth while.

Finally I'd like to thank my Mum, Pat Bell, who first showed me the world and in whose artistic footsteps I will always follow and to whom I'd like to dedicate this book.

Steve Bell
Brighton
March 1999

BELL'S EYE

Twenty Years of Drawing Blood

Steve Bell

Methuen

Published by Methuen 1999

1 3 5 7 9 10 8 6 4 2

This collection first published in the United Kingdom in 1999 by
Methuen Publishing Limited.
215 Vauxhall Bridge Road, London,
SW1V 1EJ.

Peribo Pty Ltd, 58 Beaumont Road, Mount Kuring-Gai
NSW 2080, Australia, ACN 002 273 761.
(for Australia and New Zealand)

Edited by Steve Bell and Brian Homer
Design by Homer Creative Communications

Methuen Publishing Limited Reg. No. 3543167.

A CIP catalogue record for this book is available from the British
Library.

ISBN 0 413 72540 5

Printed and bound in Great Britain by
Butler and Tanner, Frome, Somerset

Contents

Introduction

Above: Maggie's Farm Cover, *1981*

Below: Military Life, *1968*

I first started drawing in the fly leaves of books with my brother Peter in the early fifties. These were the only clear, unlined pieces of paper we could find. The fact that they were attached to weighty, dun coloured volumes was immaterial. It was a job lot of books that an elderly couple, the previous occupants of our house in Salt Hill Avenue, Slough, Bucks, England, United Kingdom, Europe, Western Hemisphere, Earth, Solar System, Galaxy X, Universe, Oblivion, had left behind, along with most of their furniture.

What we drew were the things that obsessed us: trains, war and zombies. Despite this cavalier attitude to the printed word we were by no means an illiterate household. We took the *Daily Mail, Punch, Civil Engineer, Eagle, Robin, Girl,* later *Beano* and *Beezer,* and later still *Wham!* and *Smash!* This underlying sense of blank paper being in short supply is one of the main reasons my drawings are very small, another being the fact that I am left-handed and hold a pen or pencil in such a roundabout way that my face is never more than a few inches from the page. These days I treasure and hoard pristine drawing blocks and, despite the fact that I do it for a living, as a general rule I am loth to set pencil to paper. At least not without a very good reason. These days that means earn money, have a laugh and stiff a Tory, and when you manage to do all three at once it's a good day, and if I can bring trains, war or zombies into the drawing, it's a downright briiliant day.

Learning to draw is one way of taking control over your world. If you can learn to delineate something you can, in a way, take possession of that thing and summon it up at will. This is why we drew trains. War was exciting and I dreamed of leading my platoon into battle. While walking the dog I used to frequently hurl myself into ditches, lost in heroic action fantasy. It was only a trip to the Imperial War Museum at the age of thirteen that cured me of this bizarre affliction. It was partly the accumulation of mechanised war equipment that I had expected to find exciting and in fact found grim. The thing that struck me most deeply, however, was the Paul Nash painting *Spring in the Trenches,* set like a disturbing jewel amidst all the tawdry war junk. It seemed to sum up and at the same time transcend the mess it was describing. Then there was the irony of it.

Having given up my ambition to be an army officer, or an engineer like my father (I was never any good at maths), I had by now come round to the idea of being an artist. The thing I've always liked about art is the fact that nobody knows what on earth it is, or even, if it is something, whether it is alive or dead. This means that, with a degree of self-confidence (which is of course the difficult thing to acquire) you can do whatever you like. The other good thing is that you've always got something to show for your efforts. In art lessons we drew lots of still-lives, figure compositions and suchlike; in other lessons we drew cartoons of the teachers. This for me was the birth of satire. The headmaster was called Wilf, or Paunch, and there was a German teacher called Goof who, in retrospect, looked uncommonly like John Selwyn Gummer. My friend

Paul, who could draw Prime Ministers Wilson, Home and Heath very impressively, developed the Goof character into something delightfully subversive. You can make a good, workable comic character do all sorts of unlikely and rude things. They are entirely in your power. You can get your own back on the whimsical psychopaths who run your life out there in the alleged real world.

My career as a budding artist blossomed as I made an impressive series of drawings of nearly every railway station in the South Bucks area. However it hit the buffers, so to speak, as soon as I arrived at art college in Middlesbrough. Despite a year spent doing enough life drawings to fill a medium-sized shed, I knew I wasn't getting anywhere, and worse still I was ceasing to enjoy drawing. Perhaps it was the peculiarly brow-beating teaching methods ('Forget everything you ever learned, effete southern bastard! *This* is what Art is about!'). Perhaps it was the fact that I was exiled in the North-East and all my friends were down south. Then again it may have been that I was coming to realise the utter futility and impossibility of being an 'artist'. The battles had all been fought and lost a long time ago. I had no feel for paint, and anyway, painting was pointless since Cézanne had done it all. Sculpture involved formal experiment in polystyrene and concrete and was an unmitigated pain in the arse, and as for cartooning, well, that was *illustration,* that wasn't proper art at all. These apparently fatuous and conflicting thoughts do go through your mind when you study something that doesn't seem to have a purpose for existing, other than chronic self-indulgence, and anyway, didn't we all understand that after Cubism nothing in Art would ever be the same again?

The thing that salvaged my interest in drawing was paradoxically stopping doing it altogether and then doing a course at Leeds University that had a large art and film history element, with a practical course running alongside it. At last I found a purpose for Art, which was to make posters for the Film Society. I also made posters in support of the striking miners. This was my first overtly political piece of work in that it featured a caricature of Prime Minister Edward Heath perched, along

Monsieur L'Artiste

Nobody knows what Art is
Some say it's what Artists do
But that's Shit

Above: *If...strip, 1986*

Below: *Slough Station, 1967*

with a couple of bloated capitalists, upon the shoulders of a disgruntled looking miner. The miner was wading waist-deep in something in which a sign board was placed which said 'The Shit'. A friend supplied the overall caption, 'Heading for a fall', which was magnificently prescient, bearing in mind that, owing to technical difficulties with the screen printing, the finished poster appeared just one day before the general election of 28 February 1974, which Heath did of course lose. This taught me that it's not enough just to be right, it's important to be published in time as well.

Not believing in Art I resolved to be socially useful and become a teacher. On the plus side this meant I could be a student for another year. On the minus side it meant I had to teach Art, which I didn't believe in. I survived for one year before realising that, on the whole, I preferred having my wisdom teeth pulled out. I'd been cartooning in my spare time for the magazine *Birmingham Broadside* where Brian Homer employed me for no money to produced a strip called *Maxwell the Mutant* about a man who mutated into anything from the Queen to a punk rocker whenever he drank a pint of mild. This had some satirical references to local Birmingham politicians.

After I took the plunge, packed in teaching and started to look for freelance cartoon and illustration work, the *Broadside* strip transmogrified into the story of the *Cul de Sac Motel* (my girlfriend Heather was the reason I was in Birmingham, and she and I were big *Crossroads* fans), with the evil Mag Thatcher in the Meg Richardson role. This was my first stab at a comic featuring national politicians.

Above: Bigfoot, *Arts Lab Press, 1977*

Below: Maxwell, *Broadside, 1977*

I'd long entertained a sneaking desire to be a *Beano* artist (I still have the rejection letter with the colourful *Beano* letterhead), since one of my cartoonist heroes was Leo Baxendale, the inventor of *Little Plum*, *The Bash Street Kids*, *The Three Bears*, *Minnie the Minx*, *The Banana Bunch* and, when he moved to IPC, virtually the entire contents of *Wham!* and *Smash!* comics. I'd absorbed his style from early childhood, and when I came across the American cartoonist Robert Crumb's work in my late teens, I consciously strove to draw like him, in the same sordid realist style. (I bought a Rapidograph, which kept me going for several years until it finally clogged up for the last time, switching to felt tips until I discovered that they fade away after a couple of years, when I at last made the change to dip pen and indian ink.)

The first actual paid work I got was for an IPC children's comic called *Jackpot,* where, after a lot of fruitless meetings a commissioning editor called Bob Paynter took me on for thirty weeks to write and draw a strip called *Dick Doobie,* which was an original idea about a lad with his head on back to front (and upside down to boot) and who spoke in upside down mirror writing. This made it utterly impenetrable to most of the readership, and Dick was mercifully put out of his misery when the thirty weeks were up.

Aside from the clear influence of Baxendale and Crumb, and the inspiring example of Trog, Illingworth and Searle, style is generally the name I give to my mistakes. It's also a reaction against life drawing and a celebration of anatomical incorrectness. When you start out professionally as I did with very little in the way of a body of work,

The strip below is part of a series called Fried Egg Revisited *drawn for the* Guardian's Impact *magazine in 1989. The Charles Ryder character makes the same three vows I remember making whilst still a student to (a) never get married; (b) never be a teacher; and (c) never live in Birmingham.*

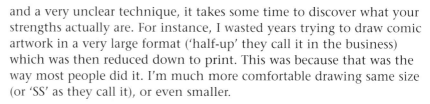

and a very unclear technique, it takes some time to discover what your strengths actually are. For instance, I wasted years trying to draw comic artwork in a very large format ('half-up' they call it in the business) which was then reduced down to print. This was because that was the way most people did it. I'm much more comfortable drawing same size (or 'SS' as they call it), or even smaller.

The other thing is noses. Some start with the eyes, some start with the mouth; I always start with the nose. The nose for me is the heart of the cartoon, but I did start my professional career with some odd forms of stylisation. This is most obvious in the *Bella the Lucky Housewife* strip which I drew for Hunt Emerson and Dave Hatton at the *Arts Lab Press* in Birmingham. The artwork was about A2 size and Bella's nose is frankly absurd. The narrative was something of a breakthrough though, since it kept taking insanely violent sideways leaps, as Bella's husband, Jack, succumbs to unexpected police machine-gun fire and Bella is arrested.

I got into trouble with Bella when she appeared in the right-on lefty newsmag the *Leveller* and was spiked by a lethal combination of pious elements ('I don't think it's the role of this magazine to poke fun at working class women, comrade.') The full page strip *Gilbert Gauche Joins the Movement* appeared in the *Leveller* at around this time. There was a large amount of ludicrous posturing on the left during the seventies, and much of it was pre-post-ironic, or tongue in cheek, but to pretend that this rag bag of dewy-eyed Trots, Anarchists and clanking Tankies ever threatened the fabric of civilisation is to accord us far more significance than we ever believed we had ourselves. Then Thatcher came along.

Left: Bella the Lucky Housewife, Birmingham Arts Lab Press, *1978*
Below: Bella the Lucky Housewife, *unpublished, 1979*
Opposite: Gilbert Gauche, The Leveller, *1978*

Thatcher's Eyeballs

The true triumph of Thatcherism was its complete rewriting of history. We think of the picture she and her allies concocted of the 'Winter of Discontent' and who can forget the queues to bury the dead and the piles of rotting rubbish? Since the image still goes largely unchallenged, you have to pinch yourself to try and remember that this was a largely mythic creation of a small number of newspaper editors. It was a good story and they plugged it for all it was worth, but it was just that – a story. The truth was far more mundane: a series of strikes in the public services against extremely low pay at a time of increasing inflation. The rest is bollocks. Thatcher no more managed to conquer inflation than Mickey Mouse or the Emperor Nero. In 1978 the inflation rate stood at 8%. When she left office in 1990 it stood at 10.5%.

What Thatcher successfully managed to do was to call the revolutionary bluff of leftist ideology and identify her own regime exclusively with the continuation of civilisation-as-we-know-it. She took the credit for everything positive. Everything negative she managed to attribute to the machinations of the trades unions and the left. The tooth-grinding, buttock-clenching, eye-watering frustration of receiving lectures on democracy from a party where nobody actually had a vote for anything took its toll on us pathological pinkos. And how to caricature something so monstrously hypocritical. That was my problem. She was blonde with a highish voice and a hectoring, lecturing manner. But before you can do a successful caricature you have to have some notion of the character underneath.

There was definitely something about those eyeballs, in particular relation to that nose and the swoop of that hairdo. *Fuck you all…* 1979 wasn't drawn for anybody in particular, but it was the first time I thought I might be getting somewhere with her caricature. It's based on the way she appeared when she purported to quote St Francis of Assisi's Prayer on the day of her accession.

Both drawings
from Maggie's Farm *book, 1981.*

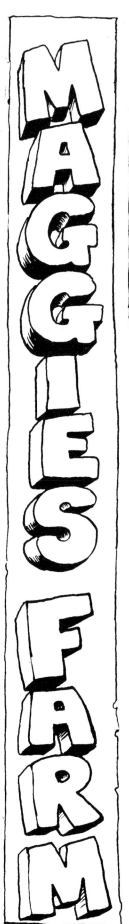

Thatcher came to power on 4 May 1979. I got taken on to do a fortnightly strip in London's Time Out magazine in June 1979. My first goes at her are really no more than reworkings of photographic references; one such is the Maggie's Farm strip which dealt with her first party conference in power in the October of that year.

I pulled out all the stops in that drawing however, pouring in as many taking-Thatcher-to-her-logical-conclusion gags as I could possibly squeeze in.

This cartoon illustrates the ending of the Iranian Embassy siege in London by the SAS in the summer of 1980. It took place live on prime-time television. Jimmy Carter's last year as President was dominated by his own Iranian hostage crisis, when the staff of the US Embassy in Tehran were held hostage by the new revolutionary Islamic government led by the Ayatollah Khomeini. Carter's failure to resolve this crisis contributed to his defeat by Ronald Reagan in the presidential election that same year.

The Maggie's Farm *above was drawn in 1981 at the height of the craze for New Romanticism. The principal characters are, left to right: Margaret Thatcher, William Whitelaw (Deputy Leader and Home Secretary), Sir Keith Joseph (Industry Secretary), Michael Heseltine (Environment Secretary), Sir Geoffrey Howe (Chancellor of the Exchequer) and James Prior (Employment Secretary). In the bottom right-hand corner are David Owen and William Rodgers, two of the original SDP Gang of Four.*

The two Maggie's Farm *cartoons on the left lampoon early moves towards privatisation by the Thatcher government. Sir Keith Joseph was Margaret Thatcher's intellectual mentor on the free-market right of the Conservative Party. It's interesting to reflect in hindsight (these were drawn in 1980-81) how yesterday's perceived madness has become today's accepted wisdom.*

The Iron Lady

Within a year of taking office
Margaret Thatcher had
consciously established a
character. This was the Iron Lady
(in itself a response to a
dismissive Soviet slur) and she
was 'not for turning'. The voice
had lowered and the hair had
stiffened and darkened. I
witnessed the moment she
delivered that phrase at first hand
from the front row (where the
press are allowed to sit) in the
Brighton Centre in October 1980.
The stiff deliberation of her
delivery meant that it made lousy
theatre, but of course, as I
discovered later, it was expertly
designed to be repeated on
television, *ad nauseam*.

The Maggie's Farm *above, from October 1980, depicts the last Labour Party conference before the SDP breakaway. Top row, left to right: Denis Healey, Tony Benn, Shirley Williams, David Owen, William Rodgers and James Callaghan.*

Hard Left

Thatcher was particularly well served by a disintegrating opposition. The machinations of the evil, and quite possibly mad, socialist demagogue, the so-called 'Tony Benn', led to the opportunistic entryism into the Labour Party of hardened lefties like me and Heather, and the principled exit of the founders of the Social Democratic Party. We entered the world of envelope-stuffing and number-taking where we plotted the overthrow of everything the British people hold dear. Our local Labour councillor became an SDP convert. He canvassed our house one day and took the trouble to harangue us on our own doorstep about the evils of the lefty Trot conspiracy. He bore an uncanny facial resemblance to the abominable Ned (later Lord) Lagg in the *If...* strip, which began life in the *The Guardian* in November 1981.

Thatcher was by this time well into her role as Iron Lady. Rocketing unemployment and swingeing cuts in public services meant that she was, if the opinion polls meant anything, the least popular prime minister this century. The fatal miscalculation the breakaway SDP made was that she would stay this way. Then along came General Galtieri.

The Falklands War
or South with Growing Disbelief

In April 1982 when the century was old, empires had come and largely gone and the world knew what wars really meant, this empire went to war. To defend itself against aggression. To defend the right of small nations to make empires out of other small nations, far away.

Where penguins swim and sheep strut and kelpers do things with kelp, the fascist Argentine invaded a brave little land sustained by cups of tea and buns, secure in the knowledge that it was owned by the Coalite Corporation, who clearly weren't interested in the fish.

A nagging doubt remained. This was one war that could have been avoided. Unfortunately the resolute approach was all the rage then, along with Royalty, New Romanticism and a certain coyness about the effects of high explosives on soldiers' bodies. We had been paying ourselves more than we had earned for far too long, and you could not blame the government.

A task force was dispatched, another war game that was to achieve new levels of realism. We had three weeks to contemplate exactly how we were going to the Malvinas, how we were going to kill a spick or two. Live, on board HMS *Canberra*, courtesy of the Ministry of Defence: a cruise in the shade of the *Sun*.

Duck designed by B.J. Homer

The Maggie's Farm *on the left was drawn as a response to a story about Argentine scrap metal dealers raising the Argentine flag on the uninhabited island of South Georgia. I was actually inking the thing up, on the Friday, 2 April 1982, when the news started to come through of the actual Argentine invasion of the Falklands. All hell broke loose, and Parliament was recalled for a special sitting on the Saturday. It authorised the sending of a task force to the South Atlantic.*

The imaginary saga of Able Seaman Reg Kipling and Commander Jack Middletar in their armoured nuclear punt was my way of coping with the insanity of the Falklands War. *The Guardian* was one of the very few papers that was prepared to publish anything that questioned the rebirth of jingo. Questions were asked in the House attacking Les Gibbard for his version of the famous Zec cartoon of World War Two: *The Price of Sovereignty Has Increased - Official.* There was a strong sense of belonging to a persecuted minority, but the response from like-minded readers was tremendous. The Penguin character turned up because the South Atlantic is where penguins do tend to turn up, but he got such fanatical fan mail that I decided to keep him on full time.

In my early days on the The Guardian *there was a gap of up to ten days between my delivering a week's worth of strips and them actually appearing in the paper. The task force was well on its way by the time the Middletar/Kipling saga appeared. Middletar is loosely based on* Dan Dare: Pilot of the Future.

H.M. GOVERNMENT TRAINING STRIP.

Lessons had clearly been learned that harrowing, uncontrolled Vietnam-style coverage was bad for morale back home, and the press output from the task force was strictly censored by the Ministry of Defence. Action pictures were particularly sparse. The Boom! Thud! Pym! *strip happened to coincide with the release of the famous picture of* HMS Antelope *exploding and was not published for reasons of taste. Everything else was. (Francis Pym was Foreign Secretary at the time.)*

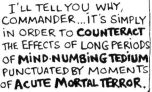

This is the first ever appearence of the Penguin in the If... *strips. These strips were published in* The Guardian *from 24-29 May 1982.*

These strips were published from 7-12 June 1982 as the ground battle for the Falkland Islands was reaching its climax.

IF....

AH WELL, BARRY, THE MILITARY KNOWS BEST!

SO IT WOULD SEEM...

YOU'LL **LEARN** THAT AS YOU **GO ALONG**, SON. YOU'LL FIND THAT **WE JOURNALISTS** ARE DEPENDENT ON THEM FOR **EVERYTHING**; **FOOD**, **DRINK**, **FAGS**, **INFORMATION**, – **THE LOT** ....

IN THAT CASE, **WHY** DO THEY **BOTHER** HAVING US HERE **AT ALL**, HARRY?

BECAUSE MR. + MRS AVERAGE PUNTER - BACK - HOME WILL **BELIEVE** WHAT <u>WE</u> TELL THEM, BECAUSE WE HAVE **JOURNALISTIC INTEGRITY**, AND A DEGREE OF **OBJECTIVITY** THE MILITARY CAN' **NEVER** PROVIDE!

YES, BUT **WHAT** DO WE **TELL** THEM??

HANG ON, I'LL ASK THE MAJOR...

IFoooo

GOOD OF YOU TO GRANT US THIS **INTERVIEW** MAJOR...

BIG·SHOW·OUR·CHAPS· MAJOR·TARGETS SOFTENED UP · SHOT·DOWN·TAKEN- -OUT·HARD·FIGHTING ·STIFF·RESISTANCE

BIG·PUSH·PINCER· ·MOVEMENT·HAMMER· ·AND·ANVIL·TRICKY·TERRAIN ·LIGHT·CASUALTIES· FRIGHTENED·CONSCRIPTS ·HOLES·IN·BOOTS· THREW·DOWN·ARMS

RETURN·TO·NORMAL OUR·LADS·WELCOME·CUPPA ·ROYAL·WEDDING·MUGS· –ARGENTINIANS– –LICK·WOUNDS!

IF....

I COULDN'T **UNDERSTAND** A GREAT DEAL OF WHAT THAT **MAJOR SAID**, HARRY...

DON'T WORRY, SON, – THAT'S **BASIC M.O.D. SPEAK**.– YOU'LL PICK IT UP AS YOU GO ALONG – IT'LL ALL MAKE **SENSE** IN GOOD TIME!

...BUT IT'S **NO USE**.... I STILL **CAN'T STOP** THINKING ABOUT THAT "**SURPRISINGLY LIGHT CASUALTY**" I SAW!.

BARRY, I DON'T QUITE KNOW HOW TO PUT THIS, BUT WHAT YOU SAW WAS...

ANY·CONFLICT REGRETTABLE·NECESSITY SUSTAIN·FATALITIES OUR·HEARTS·GO·OUT BUT·NEVER·FORGET **REASONS WHY** ALL·THIS·TAKES·PLACE –REASONS·FUNDA· –MENTAL·TO·OUR CIVILISATION

YES, HARRY, BUT **WHAT ARE** THE REASONS?

HANG ON ... I'LL ASK THE MAJOR....

Norman Tebbit replaced the 'wet' James Prior as Employment Secretary in 1981. Tebbit had a reputation as a parliamentary bruiser. Michael Foot described him as a 'badly house-trained polecat'. He gleefully pushed through increasingly punitive trades union reforms.

After the Victory

After the victory came the victory parade, which was rather more than some of our more squeamish elements could take. Everyone, save Thatcher, had lost something; whether it was Michael Foot who, having condoned the whole proceeding, lost credibility as a peace campaigner, or the SDP which lost valuable publicity and sympathetic column inches, or the armed forces who lost actual lives. The Conservative Party Conference in Brighton in October 1982 ran under the slogan 'The Resolute Approach', and a general election was called a whole year earlier than expected.

The Argentinians surrendered on 14 June 1982. Mrs Thatcher told cheering crowds in Downing Street: 'We had to do what we had to do. Great Britain is great again.'

The liner Canberra, *requisitioned for the course of the war, returned home to* Southampton *on 11 July 1982 to a tumultuous welcome. A rail strike was going on at the time.*

A parade was held through the City of London. Thatcher reviewed the troops herself in her new-found role as Head of State and Mother of the Nation.

BRITHATCHIA BANISHING THE DARK DIVISIVE CLOUDS OF MARXIST SOCIALISM FROM THE LAND...

MAGGIES FARM — ...help make this title redundant — © Steve Bell 1983

The 1983 General Election

The general election in June 1983 was between the rampant Conservatives, led by Margaret Thatcher, a less than rampant Labour Party, led by Michael Foot, and the breakaway SDP, led by Roy Jenkins, in alliance with the Liberal Party, led by David Steel. The SDP achieved its moment of immortality. We took numbers at our local polling station. I sat between an old girl for the Tories and a middle-aged bloke on behalf of the Ned Lagg character who had doorstepped us earlier. We were all perfectly friendly and polite. We had a great deal in common, sitting there outside the Baptist chapel. We were all equally out of touch with the public mood.

The SDP lost most of its MPs. We in the Labour Party hadn't done so badly since 1918 and the old girl's lot got a majority of 144 on a reduced share of the vote. Whichever way you looked at it this was a gross state of affairs.

The Militant tendency fielded a number of candidates under the Labour banner, and one Tory candidate was shown to have had connections with the National Front.

The Special Relationship

Ronald Reagan, elected to the Presidency in November 1980, was Margaret Thatcher's ideological soulmate. She had read all his speeches and agreed with them all. She described herself as 'his principal cheerleader in NATO'.

Left: *Margaret Thatcher was always pro-hanging, yet even at this, her victorious height, in a free vote in a House of Commons bursting at the seams with Tories, there was never sufficient support for its return. Left to right along the bottom: Leon Brittain (Home Secretary); Nigel Lawson (Chancellor of the Exchequer who, in spite of this cartoon, was actually opposed to capital punishment); and Norman Tebbit. (After* The Swing, *by Fragonard).*
Above: *Drawn for the* New Statesman, *1986*

Big Ron

Ronald Reagan saw everything in global or hemispheric terms, depending whether he was in the mood to dominate the entire world or only half of it. He spoke out against 'big government' yet engineered the biggest government spending spree (on armaments) in human history. His creed was simple: a belief in the elect who would literally be spirited up to Heaven ('the Rapture') when 'Tribulation' struck. Since he was uniquely in a position to bring about such a state of affairs, this

must have given him an exceptional feeling of personal spiritual security. He saw the Soviet Union as an 'Evil Empire' and the United States as a 'Shining City on a Hill'. Everywhere else was either a source of raw materials or a place to park a missile. In a land given to self-mythologising he was God's gift and they loved him for it. He was re-elected by a landslide in 1984. Fortunately the American Constitution prevented him from standing for a third term, about which he did grumble, before his poor old brain finally gave out. There are now serious proposals to carve his head on Mount Rushmore.

Drawn for City Limits, *30 September 1985.*

The Dream Ticket

Michael Foot stood down as Labour leader in October 1983 to make way for the 'dream ticket' of Neil Kinnock and Roy Hattersley. The day that the results were announced in the conference hall in Brighton, I was standing at the back spectating. (It was ridiculously easy to get into party conferences in those pre-Brighton bombing days.) A bearded bloke came up to me and asked if he could borrow my CND badge 'for Glenys'. It was a particularly nice shiny badge made of that rainbow refracting plastic (the sort compact discs are made of) which was all the rage then. I was nonplussed, but happy to oblige so I let him have it. Sure enough, when the result was announced on came Neil and Glenys Kinnock waving and, if my memory serves me right, flinging roses into the applauding multitude, and there was my shiny badge pinned on her red dress. I never saw it again.

Space constraints mean that the full story of the penguins has been cut short. The Penguin, having moved in with Kipling in a flat in Peckham, is presented with an egg by Gloria, with whom he had a fling during the 1983 election campaign, and told to get on with it. Cousin King, who lost his quiff along with all his other feathers while doing post-war salvage work for the Ministry of Defence in the Falklands, has become radically disaffected, as well as gay, and shares the flat.

The first US Cruise missiles arrived to be stationed in Britain towards the end of 1983. There were massive demonstrations against their arrival in central London and in other European cities.

Strange Times

These were strange times. Apparently Tony Blair was a CND member. They let anybody in in those days. Michael Heseltine was Defence Secretary, taking care to be photographed in a very fetching combat jacket, and cruise missiles were set to arrive at Greenham Common in the autumn of 1983. The women's peace camp there brought the full obscenity of these battlefield nuclear weapons into focus.

Monsieur L'Artiste couldn't see what all the fuss is about. The strip about each day being 'like a rebirth' was lifted almost verbatim from a radio interview with Jean-Michel Jarre I happened to hear at the time.

*With unchallenged power and a huge majority came heightened paranoia.
Margaret Thatcher's attention turned towards imagined subversion, the
suppression of trade unions at GCHQ, and the 'Enemy Within'.*

Her direct dealings with the media were strictly rationed, and the only radio programme she seemed willing to appear on was the Jimmy Young show on BBC Radio 2, where she felt she could address her own supporters without any impertinent interrogator getting in the way.

RUNNING REPAIRS ON THE IRON LADY

— Apologies to Stanley Spencer R.A.

© Steve Bell 1983

Solidarity

There are problems being an artist and a small businessman - atomised individualist that I am - believing in justice and trade unionism, with no shop floor to speak of. It's not a new phenomenon but it's growing alarmingly, though it's far too late to be alarmed.

During the 1972 miners' strike we cheered from the sidelines. We were students, we needed to unite with the workers. During the 1974 strike we undertook voluntary work in support of the miners. This involved taking baked beans at dead of night to a picket line at a colliery in Elland. 'I've been listening to Radio Moscow', I chirped - aged 22, hair down to my armpits - to a real miner. 'And you're a twat.' He was too polite to say this, but his look spoke volumes.

I joined the National Union of Teachers (NUT) in 1976. I was an art teacher in Birmingham, and not a terribly good one. The fact was I didn't want to be there. I hated the staff, the school and most of the pupils. After the collapse of the pound and the International Monetary Fund loan in 1976 the cuts started in earnest. I wore a badge to school on my tweed lapel which said 'Stop the Cuts'. That's the way we used to communicate in those days. I knew there had to be a better way, so I fucked off to be a cartoonist and joined the National Union of Journalists (NUJ).

The miners' strike of 1984-85 saw a concerted move to implement the new, restrictive, trade union legislation. 'Flying pickets' and any form of sympathetic industrial action not directly connected to your own place of work had become illegal. This effectively meant the end of freedom of movement around the country for anybody resembling a miner.

Police from all round the country were deployed in mining areas. Unfortunately the NUM was split right from the outset of the strike between a majority who wanted to strike to prevent further pit closures and a minority who did not wish to strike and resented the fact that no ballot on national strike action had been called. Attempts to 'picket out' these objectors were frustrated in the early days of the dispute, and the union eventually split completely.

APOLOGIES TO FATS WALLER, AND APOLOGIES TO FATS DOMINO FOR APOLOGISING TO FATS WALLER BY MISTAKE LAST TIME — I JUST GOT MY FATS WRONG, THAT'S ALL.

The NUM had its funds sequestered and police action was coordinated nationally to keep the strike's effects to a minimum. Techniques included the deployment of troops in police uniforms and the siege and occupation of areas loyal to the union.

The Flying Pickets

In 1984 I got talking to some flying pickets outside Shoreham power station. They were happy to talk and we as a family were happy to support them in any way we could. It was important that they won, but I had doubts, guilty doubts, for I was a freelance working for a national paper (*The Guardian*), which on the surface appears to be a denial of solidarity: selling my services to the highest bidder, indeed to the only bidder available under the circumstances.

We gave what we could. We put a couple of miners up for long periods for the entire period of the strike. We sold loads of artwork to raise money, for there was a strike to be won and all the wrong things, the false stories, were making the headlines. 'Don't worry, if you're not prepared to talk to us we'll just make it up anyway', a reporter assured one of the miners staying with us.

The fact was that the government was out to destroy the National Union of Miners. After a year, as the 'drift back to work' accelerated and they finally marched back to work, unbeaten, heads held high, bands playing, without even a ghost of a settlement, we tried to offer some form of hope as comfort to our miners, one of whom said despairingly, 'We fucking lost.'

That same year Rupert Murdoch sacked his union workforce in Fleet Street and set up shop inside Fortress Wapping in London's Docklands.

Irish Myth and Legend Part One

The troubles in Northern Ireland had been going on since 1969, when the agitation for civil rights for the Catholic nationalist population turned into something far more ugly and intractable. After the invasion of the Catholic areas by the infamous 'B' special police auxiliaries, who, back in 1969, pushed through a policy of what would now be described as 'ethnic

cleansing', the security forces have been regarded as part of the problem, but only by one side of the community. The above strips refer to a miraculous wobbling statue of the Madonna that was in the news at the time (1985).

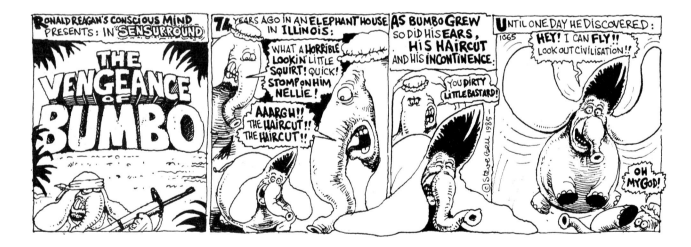

The Israelis, under the right-wing Likud Prime Minister Menachem Begin, invaded the Lebanon in June 1982 to drive out the Palestine Liberation Organisation. Yasser Arafat, the PLO leader, finally left Beirut to set up new headquarters in Tunisia in August 1982. Rather than solving their terrorist problem, the Israeli invasion seemed rather to enhance it. New, more fanatical organisations came to the fore. One such led a suicide-bombing attack on the headquarters of the US and French peacekeeping forces in October 1983.

241 US Marines and 58 French paratroopers were killed. Ronald Reagan responded by invading Grenada, a small island in the Caribbean with a Marxist-led government. The operation was a resounding success, and the Marxists were overthrown. The top two strips on the left (from 1985) refer to an incident where just before a TV broadcast, Reagan joked with cameramen: 'Ladies and gentlemen: tonight we bomb Russia!'

Star Wars

Reagan first introduced his 'Star Wars' or - Strategic Defense Initiative - to the world early in 1983. He claimed his proposals, to zap incoming missiles in space with laser beams, microwaves and whatever else the industry could dream up, would make nuclear weapons 'impotent and obsolete', but not before they had given a huge boost to arms spending.

Reagan met Mikhail Gorbachev, the new Soviet leader, at a summit meeting in Geneva in November 1985.

The world's worst civil nuclear disaster (as far as we know) took place at Chernobyl in the Ukraine in April 1986, when the reactor caught fire and huge amounts of radioactivity escaped from its exposed core. A plume of radioactivity went round the world. High rainfall in the Pennines at the time meant that the radioactive contamination got into the food chain. Laz and Larry are probably still inedible to this day.

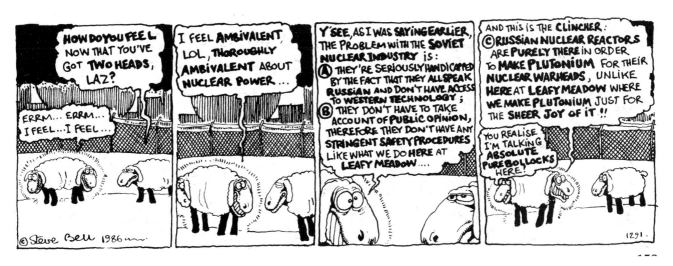

The Euro-bomb was one of the favoured policy options of the Liberal SDP Alliance. The idea of having a short-sighted whale interfere with the deterrent came unbidden one day and the strips virtually drew themselves while I sniggered uncontrollably.

This was the cover of Frustrate Their Knavish Tricks *by Ben Pimlott (1994).*

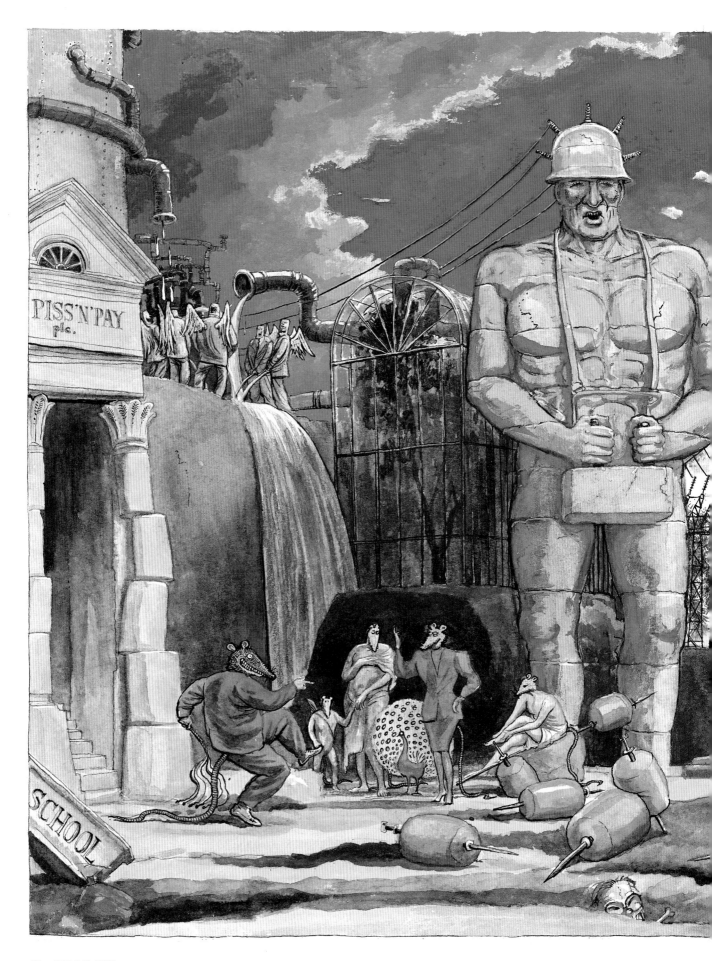

Cecil Parkinson - Conservative Party Chairman 1981-83, Trade & Industry Secretary 1983, matinée idol, nuclear-powered stud, friend of Norman Tebbit, favourite of Margaret Thatcher, victim of shag-and-tell by former secretary, mother of daughter - spent four years in the wilderness, then returned as Energy Secretary in 1987.

The original title of this pastiche of Claude Lorraine and Nicholas Poussin, drawn for the New Statesman *in January 1989, was:* Landscape with Monuments to a Vanished Civilisation, Kebab Herds, Lager Louts, Raunch Generator and Parking for 50 Billion Cars.

The Wonderful World of Colour

In late 1987 *New Society* magazine was absorbed by the *New Statesman*. *New Society* had always been a good magazine to work for, since they paid good rates, always sent you your artwork back and always invited contributors to a very congenial piss-up at Christmas. Stuart Weir, who became editor of *New Statesman & Society* (as it remained for a year or two) asked me to supply a weekly half-page cartoon in full colour. It was a great opportunity, but colour had never been my strong point. Anything too far beyond grass-is-green and pillar-boxes-are-red and I would get stuck. I applied myself to the task, and came to spend many happy hours doing miniature watercolour versions of famous Pre-Raphaelite paintings. I set out to find out exactly why their moral contents were so lurid and their colours were so vivid. It was here that I discovered that the wonderful world of colour, rather like the world of late-eighties politics, is suffused with blue.

104.9.4.90 ~~~   — © Steve Bell 1990 —

Above: *The eighties saw a massive increase in the prison population with little improvement in the fabric of prisons. Strangeways Prison was gutted by rioting prisoners in 1990. The Home Secretary at the time was David Waddington, to whom the above cartoon bears an uncanny resemblance.*

Left: *Early moves towards prison privatisation drawn in 1988 after the famous image from* London - a Pilgrimage *by Gustave Doré.*

Overleaf left: *The heir to the throne has always taken a close interest in architecture. We have him to thank for the National Gallery extension, one of the nastiest public buidings in London. This is an imaginary replacement for the Bull Ring in Birmingham. Drawn in November 1988.*

Overleaf right: *Kenneth Baker was Education Secretary from 1986-89. He introduced most of the key reforms that have dominated the educational agenda ever since, including the National Curriculum, Standard Attainment Tests, league tables, opting out of schools from local authorities and indeed everything except increased funding or smaller class sizes. Drawn in March 1989.*

Campanile (Height restricted to 365 ft in Harmony with St. Pauls.)

Discreetly Tasteful Neon Signs

Monarchy
Plutocracy
Hereditary Landlordism
you know they make sense

Classical Gazebo Retailing Environment designed for Birmingham City Centre by H.R.H. the Prince of Wales

To be constructed using only the finest Traditional Vernacular Materials (Wattle, Daub, Pork Scratchings) and clad in Gloucestershire Stone.

Umbrella Vaulting in Cranial Atrium

Cantilever Earspan

Window to the Soul

Ear Section

Plan

Giant Sight Screen to cover depressingly Soul-less Vista of Sixties Lay-Cost Ryuecil Hyzing (To be carved with Scalloped Curlicues by products of closed-down Art Courses or Y.T.S. trainees, whichever do be cheaper.)

THE BULL RING

Ghastly Bolognaise of Visual Unpleasantness

Architecturally integrated Shop Signs

Gino's Gino's Tesco Tesco Tesco Next Next Next

Peter Brooke as The Man Who Suggested the Distant Hypothetical Possibility of a Political Settlement in Northern Ireland. *This is the closest I have ever come to a pro-Tory government cartoon. It was drawn for the* New Statesman *in November 1989 in the style of H.M. Bateman.*

Irish Myth and Legend Part Two

A low-intensity war continued in Northern Ireland throughout the eighties. Thatcher's policy of no compromise with the men of violence – at least the ones on the republican side – combined with an attempt to impose the Anglo-Irish Agreement and the principle of Irish government involvement in Northern Irish Affairs met with little success.

Then in 1989 Peter Brooke, the Northern Ireland Secretary (1989-92) hinted that there was the ghost of a possibility that a political settlement could be conceived of that did actually involve the participation of, or perhaps even contact with, representatives of Sinn Fein. There was the predictable outraged response from Unionists of all shades.

Drawn for the New Statesman *in May 1989, this cartoon of Thatcher with her son, daughter-in-law and grandson was based on a photomontage by John Heartfield and a news photograph.*

We are a Grandmother

Thatcher's High Period lasted seven years, from 1983 to 1990, but somehow it felt like twenty. By 1987 the rivets were starting to drop out, but she still managed to win another general election, albeit after a slightly wobbly campaign, with a thumping majority. This paved the way for Mad Period Thatcher, when the obscene Poll Tax (or Community Charge as the Conservatives preferred to call it) began to loom larger and larger.

The Seven Ages of Thatch

All the world's a grocer's
And all the men and women merely customers
They make their payments and their purchases
One grocer's daughter counts the cost of all
Her life being seven ages. At first
A doe-eyed, blonde-haired softie, hoarding cans
And then the shrieking minister, snatching milk
Flushed and oddly hesitant, unwont to rule
And then the Leader, sighing like a furnace
Quoting St Francis from between two cops
Eyes flashing side to side, then a warrior
Full of strange clanks, hairdo a tin box
Fighting at one remove, in a bunker
Seeking the bubble reputation
Even in the penguin's mouth. And then the ayatollah
Clad in black with boat-shaped hat of death

"Up Shit Creek" after Millais

54·5·3·89   —ⓒSteve Bell 1989

Proud eyes aswerve and neck of solid brass
Full of mad laws and new poll taxes
Until she lost her job. The sixth age shifts
Into the gaunt and haggard raving loon
Eyeballs that swivel independently
Beneath her nose, atop her scrawny neck
Charging a fortune to gaga colonials
Who want to hear an old age pensioner squeak
Hoarding applause. Last age of all
That ends this strange eventful history
All things must go, a closing clearance
Sold phones, sold gas, sold health, sold everything

The half-demolished shell of London's Battersea power station, a listed building that isn't really a building anymore, stands accusingly on the south side of the Thames; a near perfect metaphor for what eleven years of Thatcher's rule did to the country. At the time this drawing was made in 1990, the entrepreneur who was supposed to be turning the power station into a massive theme park had just pulled out of the project.

It is based on The Persistence of Memory *by Salvador Dali. My version is called* The Persistence of Wandsworth.

127 · 29 · 10 · 90 — THE GOLDEN SCENARIO — © Steve Bell 1990

The Fall

As the autumn of 1990 drew on the signs of disaffection within the Tory party became more and more obvious. Since a party in power always talks to itself in code, the ostensible grumblings were about Europe, which the electorate couldn't give two farts about, rather than the Poll Tax which was driving everybody to distraction. Thatcher's isolation became evident when she demoted her faithful sidekick Sir Geoffrey ('Dead Sheep') Howe - the last survivor apart from herself of the 1979 Cabinet - from Foreign Secretary to mere Deputy Leader, and he eventually resigned. His resignation speech, where he tore into her behaviour during negotiations on Europe, provided the pretext for Michael Heseltine, who had resigned as Defence Secretary after serious disagreements with Thatcher in 1986, to stand against her in a leadership election. She duly won that election, but by an insufficient margin to prevent it going to a second ballot. She was persuaded by her fellow ministers that she could not be sure of winning such a ballot, so she stood down in order to permit a candidate she approved of to win against the hated Heseltine. John Major, who had been Chancellor since 1989 and had recently replaced Howe as Foreign Secretary, was her favoured choice. The parliamentary party clearly agreed with her and John Major duly triumphed, beating Michael Heseltine into second and Douglas Hurd into third place.

Above: an imagined scene of what Tory MPs really wanted, drawn in late October 1990.
Top right: The Stalking Sheep, drawn a week later after Howe had resigned.
Bottom right: The Scapegoat, after Holman Hunt, drawn 19 November. She resigned on Thursday 22 November.

This cartoon was drawn for the cover of the Christmas edition of Private Eye *in 1992. Clockwise around the Unholy Madonna and child from the top left: Kenneth Clarke; Saddam Hussein; Mark Thatcher; Michael Heseltine; Malcolm Rifkind; Denis Thatcher; Lord (Cecil) Parkinson; Lord (Geoffrey) Howe; David Mellor; Norman Tebbit and Norman Lamont.*

Back to the Past

But this book is getting ahead of itself, and we must return to the high days of Thatcher prior to the general election of 1987 when everything was still black and white.

The Docklands Development Corporation was set up, independent of and not responsible to local authorities or elected representatives of the people who actually lived there, to develop a new commercial centre in the Isle of Dogs. This is what became Canary Wharf and its famous 'Penis Tower'.

Docklands 1987

There is a happy land beside a river basin where people in big trousers and dark stockings come to breed. Classless and classbound, young and ageless they come down here to do what must be done.
'What's the problem? Do you not like money? Cellphones? Wine bars? Status? Fun?'
'Privatisation - what a wheeze! Who needs corruption? Who needs sleaze?'
'We're the future, that's a matter of fact, our tongues are brown and our heads are flat.'
'It's not all good - it can be fairly shitty. You might end up with negative equity.'

The 1987 Election

The Conservatives, under the chairmanship of Norman Tebbit, had a wobbly election campaign. A newly image-conscious Labour Party, under the direction of Peter 'Red Rose' Mandelson, ran a very tight and successful campaign, setting aside for a moment the fact that they lost by an only slightly less massive margin than in 1983. The problem was still the

SDP/Liberal Alliance under the joint leadership of David Owen and David Steel which, as well as effectively splitting the opposition vote across the country, was starting to disintegrate from within.

Victory Number Three

The 1987 election is a classic example of an election where the electorate didn't read the small print. They thought they were voting for increasing prosperity, booming house prices, free money, and more sex on television. Margaret Thatcher obviously thought they were voting for the Poll Tax.

Scotland the Lucky

The Scots weren't quite so stupid. They had consistently failed to support the Tories in every election since 1979. This one was no exception. Their reward was to have the Poll Tax imposed on them a whole year before anybody else.

The Breaking of the Wind

The markets had been rising steadily all through the eighties. Britain was better off with the Conservatives, or at least Britain's better off were better off. This lent Thatcherism its invulnerable quality. Then, in the early morning of 16 October 1987 the Great Wind struck the south and east of England. The flatheads who ran the markets couldn't get into the City because trees were in the way, so the market caught a cold and took a nose dive.

Bottom left: *When gas was privatised there was a massive advertising campaign on the theme: 'Don't forget to tell Sid' (ie: 'What a fabulous deal these gas shares are for you ordinary low class types!'). Alexis (played by Joan Collins) was a leading character in* Dynasty, *a classy American soap.*

Below: *The British Petroleum (BP) sell-off was badly hit by the market crash.*

Above and right: *Thatcher took her role as Mother of the Nation very seriously. She took great trouble to visit the victims of terrorist atrocities or terrible accidents in hospital. She even had a special boat-shaped black hat for such occasions. This approach achieved new levels of bad taste when she visited the site of the King's Cross Underground Station fire in November 1987 and actually started directing the cameras round the still warm ashes of the flash fire that had killed thirty people.*

In November 1987 the IRA exploded a bomb at a Remembrance Day parade at Enniskillen in Northern Ireland, killing eleven people.

Inflation is Dead! Long Live Inflation!

Nigel Lawson, Chancellor of the Exchequer since 1983, had a weight problem. He also had an inflation problem, which he famously described as 'a blip'. As it turned out the blip lasted longer than he did, as he resigned in 1989 and inflation didn't come back under control until well into the nineties.

*The idea for the above sequence owes a great deal to Tex Avery's wonderful
animated cartoon* King Size Canary.

Channon the Useless Engine had come off the rails again.

"Ooer!" he said, "Here comes the Fat Controller!"

"What a tirrible tregedy," said the Fat Controller, "Where are the television cameras? This is all your fault," she told a passing stretcher case, "A person could get killed on this clapped ite excuse for a railway system!"

The passengers and crew all looked shamefaced.

"That's why I'll be sticking to my Motor in future!" she announced severely.

1

Nigel the Fat Engine had fallen into Shit Creek again.

"Doesn't worry me a bit," he said, "I like it here!"

Just then the Fat Controller came along in her motor boat.

"Hello Nigel, everything going swimmingly?" she asked.

"We're getting there, ma'am" said Nigel.

"How are the passengers taking it?" she asked.

"Screw the passengers!" they both laughed.

2

The passengers in Nigel the Fat Engine's train were getting rather upset.

"When is this train going to get out of Shit Creek and start moving in the right direction?" asked one.

"The train is moving in the right direction," said the Fat Controller, "it just hasn't been explained to you properly yet. Look at that!" the Fat Controller continued, pointing at a lump of ordure floating past, "See how steadily we're progressing!"

"But..but...the turd's moving not us!" spluttered the passenger as the carriage gurgled and sank.

"That's given them food for thought." beamed the Fat Controller.

3

Above and right: *Nigel the Fat Engine owes rather a lot to The Reverend W. Awdry's* Railway Series, *illustrated by C. Reginald Dalby. Paul Channon was Transport Minister at the time (1989).*

There was a knock on the window of Nigel the Fat Engine's semi-submerged carriage.

"Would you like to buy a share in Shit Creek plc?" asked the Fat Controller.

"No I most certainly would not!" snapped an angry passenger.

"It's going to cost you anyway. Improved standards cost money, you know." said the Fat Controller.

"Improved standards?!?" exploded the passenger, "You wouldn't know an improved standard from a hole in the ground!"

"Who told you about our bold new Employment Training Drainage Initiative? Are you psychic or something?" The Fat Controller seemed surprised.

4

16·3·2086 —

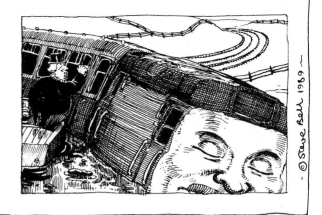

"This is a very bad railway!" said the angry passenger on Nigel the Fat Engine's train.

"Why do you think I travel everywhere by motor?" snapped back the Fat Controller, "I hate railways! You can buy the whole bang-shoot if you want!"

"I thought we owned it already - anyway we haven't got any money!" said the passenger.

"But I know a man who has!" quipped the Fat Controller.

"Guten tag, Fat Controller-san, où est le papier?" It was Jean-Gerdt Anumoto, the Euro-Japanese Venture Capitalist.

5

17 3·2087 —

"Beep Beep Allo Allo," said Jean-Gerdt Anumoto, the Euro-Japanese Venture Capitalist, "Ah will take ze entire railway urff your 'ands for a smurl consideration and Ah will buy Sheet Crick plc as well."

"A Saviour has come!" The Fat Controller gazed skyward thankfully.

"Ah 'ave only deux conditions," continued Jean-Gerdt, "You can kip the sheet and Ah will get rid of the trains."

"Done!" said a grateful Fat Controller, "That makes sound economic and ecological sense to me."

6

18·3·2088 —

Deep Shit

The sewers were falling apart, so what better idea than to sell off water and encourage people to 'Be an H_2O owner'. Carl and Carla the two yuppies are committed to life lived through an *Innovations* catalogue. One of the most noxious features of late-eighties living was the coming of 'Green Consumerism'.

The Green Party actually did very well in the Euro elections of 1989, getting 15% of the popular vote. However, there being no PR, they didn't get any seats. The other parties took fright nonetheless and started making green noises.

WELL NANCE, I GUESS IT'S GETTIN' NEAR THE TIME WHEN WE SADDLE ON UP AND MOVE ON OUT!

24·10·1976

LOOK AT THAT SUNSET!!

IT'S BEEN A GREAT EIGHT YEARS, NANCE — THIS IS A WONDERFUL COUNTRY!

I STILL CAN'T BELIEVE I'VE GOT AWAY WITH IT ALL!!

© Steve Bell 1988

Y'KNOW — I THINK I'VE DISCOVERED SOMETHING ABOUT AMERICA WHICH I NEVER REALISED BEFORE...

14·10·1977

IT'S THE ONLY PLACE ON GOD'S EARTH WHERE A MAN CAN DO WHAT A MAN'S GOTTA DO, NOT BECAUSE HE'S A MAN...

WHAT'RE YOU DRIVING AT, RON?

© Steve Bell 1988

...NOT BECAUSE HE'S EVIL OR HE'S GOOD, OR BECAUSE HE'S STUPID OR HE'S SMART, NOR EVEN BECAUSE HE'S RICH — IT'S NOT ENOUGH TO BE RICH, NANCY...

BUT RON — SURELY A MAN'S GOTTA BE RICH!?!

SURE NANCY, A MAN'S GOTTA BE RICH — BUT HE'S ALSO GOT TO BE CUTE!!

YOU MEAN - CUTE AS IN SMART?

I MEAN CUTE AS IN LITTLE STUFFED BUNNIES, NANCY

I'M DAMN PROUD OF THIS GREAT COUNTRY, NANCY — ONLY HERE IS A MAN GUARANTEED THE CONSTITUTIONAL RIGHT TO CHOOSE EVERY FOUR YEARS....

...WHETHER HE QUACKS TOUGH LIKE DONALD DUCK OR SQUEAKS FALSETTO LIKE MICKEY MOUSE. THE AMERICAN PEOPLE WILL FORGIVE ANYTHING, NANCY....

...THEY'LL FORGIVE MASS MURDER, LEGALISED THEFT, TRADE WITH THE DEVIL, LYING AND DRUG-RUN-ING. BUT ONE THING THEY WILL NEVER FORGIVE...

© Steve Bell 1988

—THEY WILL NEVER FORGIVE SOMEONE FOR NOT BEING CUTE!

DUKAKIS

26·10·1988

Creepers Into the Sunset

The Reagan era came to an end in November 1988 when George Bush, Reagan's Vice President, was elected President over the Democratic hopeful Michael Dukakis. Bush's running mate was Dan Quayle, known to posterity as the man who couldn't spell potato.

As well as being a former Director of the CIA, Bush was distinguished by a whining, quacky voice. It was rumoured that Ron used to address George as 'Whiny'.

The 'Stealth' bomber, which was being developed at the time, was the most expensive aircraft in the history of extremely expensive aircraft.

Right: *part of a* New Statesman *cartoon from November 1988, based on* American Gothic *by Grant Wood.*

Driving on with Reform

One of Thatcher's most lastingly dysfunctional reforms was that of the National Health Service, whereby what had been the public property of the NHS was handed over to numerous NHS Trusts across the country and an 'internal market' was introduced. This giant step towards bureaucratisation was piloted through by Kenneth Clarke, in the face of

the outright opposition of anybody who worked for the service, from
the trade unions and nursing organisations through to that hotbed of
bolshie radicalism, the British Medical Association (BMA). In 1990 the
ambulance workers were in dispute with the NHS.

New Order, No Credit Given

In the autumn of 1989 the Berlin Wall came down. The Soviet Union withdrew support from its satellite regimes in Eastern Europe and they fell, one by one. You could argue that Ron and Mag had won the Cold War through remaining resolute in the face of Soviet aggression, or you could argue that they were a pair of war-hungry, swivel-eyed psychos

and we are extremely lucky that the person they were facing down blinked and turned away. They did make the world safe for rotting hulks though.

Where's the Beef? Who let the Beef escape?

The first Mad Cow outbreak took place in 1989-90. It was suggested that Bovine Spongiform Encephalopathy (BSE) was a direct result of feeding cattle with the ground-up remains of demented sheep. John Selwyn Gummer, the Minister of Agriculture, refused to believe this

and publicly fed his young daughter with a burger to prove to the world it was safe. His reasoning seemed to be that he had had shit for brains all his life and it had never done him any harm. The inspiration for *The Mad Cats* came from fears that BSE could jump species.

The Desert Song

At the beginning of August 1990, Saddam Hussein invaded Kuwait. Despite the fact that the Western powers had largely supported him in the eight-year war that followed his invasion of Iran in 1980, Saddam became Global Enemy Number One overnight. The difference was oil. Saddam stood to control far too much of it, so he had to be stopped. Human rights wasn't the issue. He'd been torturing and murdering his people for years and nobody had so much as batted an eyelid. He even got away with wiping out an entire Iraqi Kurdish village with nerve gas during the long conflict with Iran. Disapproval had been expressed, nothing more.

This time the full force of the Allies was backed by a United Nations Resolution to impose a complete economic and trade embargo on Iraq. Saudi Arabia needed bolstering against possible invasion, so the 82nd Airborne Division was dispatched there. War, fiendish villains, romantic hero (George Bush): the stage was set for the final drama. I had no idea at the time that *The Desert Song* was Thatcher's favourite musical.

Once again the lessons of the Falklands War were taken on board. All coverage was to be strictly controlled. The only coverage that was not severely constrained, paradoxically, was the CNN live feed from the Al Rashid Hotel roof in Baghdad. Camels viewed through night-sights seemed to be a recurring motif.

Blackpool 1990

This is the first time I covered a party conference somewhere other than Brighton. I learnt far more about the press, including my own paper, than I did about politics. There wasn't much of that, since presentation was now everything. Kinnock was as short on content and long on verbiage as ever, though I did find out more about his body language. He turned out to be a podium-shagger. Despite the fact that the Tories were tearing themselves apart, Labour did not seem confident of victory.

Bournemouth 1990

The atmosphere in Bournemouth was of wholly inappropriate triumphalism. I'll never forget young Michael Portillo, with his old schoolboy hairdo, announcing that the Community Charge would ultimately prove 'a vote winner' for the party. Nonetheless, you didn't have to be clairvoyant to spot the fact that a lot of the representatives on the conference floor were very worried indeed. The problem wasn't Europe or Saddam Hussein (who had recently invaded Kuwait). It was the Poll Tax. Thatcher gave her closing speech to the usual rapture. People stamped and cheered, but through the glazed looks (representatives at Conservative conferences always look like they have been freshly varnished), you could sense apprehension. This was a result of what was happening outside in the wide world where riots or near-riots were happening in such inner-city hell holes as Shepton Mallet and Maidenhead. The party representatives were aware of it, the leaders clearly weren't.

Here I discovered what spin doctors did and that a 'goat fuck' is a gathering of photographers, equipped with aluminium stepladders, awaiting some great personage or event. I also learnt that a 'hamster fuck' consists of a group of political journalists, without cameras or ladders, huddled around a spin doctor, being told the story.

By-Election and Bye-Bye

Within a week or so Eastbourne, one of the safest Tory seats, had fallen in a by-election to the Liberal Democrats (whose new bird logo Thatcher, incongruously quoting from Monty Python in her conference speech, had dismissed as 'a dead parrot'). Within six weeks Margaret Thatcher herself had gone, ostensibly because she fell out with her former Foreign Secretary, Sir Geoffrey Howe, over the issue of Europe but, in fact, because of the Poll Tax and her party's very sound instincts for self-preservation.

Above: *Drawn on the day of her resignation, Thursday 22 November 1990, (left to right): Michael Heseltine, Geoffrey Howe, Douglas Hurd and John Major. Heseltine publicly called for a pause in the leadership campaign to contemplate the achievements of Margaret Thatcher.*

Below: *The so-called Sophisticated Electorate refers to the Tory MPs who were the only people allowed to vote in the leadership election.*

Major's Underpants

I first saw John Major at Thatcher's last party conference at Bournemouth in 1990. He had been Chancellor of the Exchequer since Nigel Lawson's departure a year before and was fresh from taking the country into the European Exchange Rate Mechanism (ERM). He was smiling, confident, and spoke (quite eloquently I thought, though would never have dreamed of saying so at the time) of the fact that he owed everything to the 'free enterprise capitalist system'.

But it was the nature of his upper lip that fascinated me. John Major appears to have an ingrowing moustache. That's the only thing I can think of to explain the peculiar way his upper lip seems to surround his front teeth.

After Thatcher's demise I was faced with having to draw Major a lot, and there didn't seem to be a great deal to go on. The more you studied him, the less there appeared to be to him. Looking at his record he seemed to be closely implicated in most of the truly spectacular cock-ups of the Thatcher era. He'd never raised so much as a whisper against the Poll Tax and the two things he'd been primarily responsible for, the cold weather payments to pensioners fiasco and the entry into the ERM, were not achievements to crow about. The answer to my problem was simple: John Major was not very good. In fact, he was crap.

The two-page story *Son of Kong* (pages 112 & 113) was drawn for the new Saturday *Guardian* Weekend section in early December 1990, only a couple of weeks after he came to power, and the underpants outside the trousers motif came perfectly logically out of the Superman (or in this case, Superuselessman) parody format. Superman wears sleek red briefs over blue tights. John Major wears classic aertex Y-fronts over a dark grey business suit.

I didn't pursue the underpant theme until I got some positive feedback from the *Son of Kong* strip. In the *If...* strip I was still drawing Major as a poodle, based on a joke of Roger Woddis's that 'John is very much his own poodle.' Then I read the rumour, in a Simon Hoggart piece in the *Observer*, that John Major tucks his shirt into his underpants, and I realised that there had to be some kind of mystical connection between John Major and his pants. I proceeded to flog the motif for all it was worth.

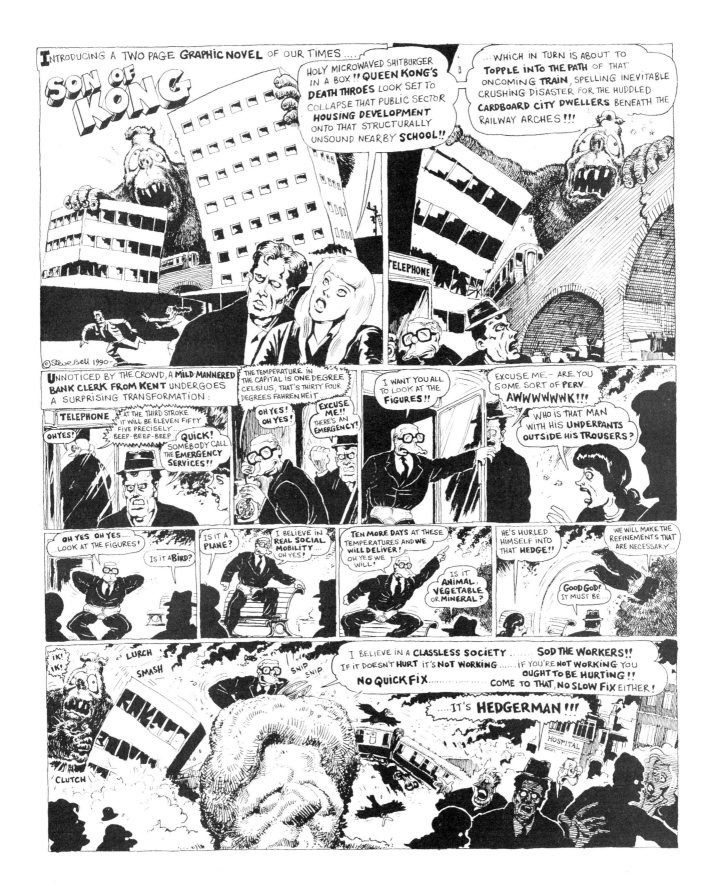

Above: Shades of World War One: *troops await the start of the ground war, February 1991.*

The Gulf War

John Major had a good war. His low-key, unhectoring manner was somehow appropriate to this overblown - though under-reported - video game of a war. The lessons of Vietnam and the Falklands were well-learnt. War needs to be on prime-time, but minus the nasty bits. The real-time idiocy of CNN came into its own during the war. John Major visited the troops in a particularly cuddly looking woolly jumper.

The battles won, the bodies bulldozed, the world went on as before. I find it hard to forget, however, just how worrying a time it had been. The potential for utter catastrophe was always there. It was catastrophic for the people of Iraq, screwed by a dictator and fucked by international sanctions, but their needs have never played a significant part in shaping the policy of the Allies.

Above: Drawn for The Guardian, *February-March, 1991.*

Top: *The ground war was intense (at least for the Iraqis) and short: it was all over by the end of February.*

Above: *Major rampant. As well as his special powers, Major has a way with the language that is all his own.*

Major's Lip

I was still grappling with the problem of Major's lip. It developed a life of its own and spread outwards, becoming more and more duck-like. I realised I was overdoing it when I saw a photograph of him in profile and noticed that, in fact, it swoops inwards around the teeth, and his chin sticks out underneath. I amended the caricature and he stayed that way, more or less, until the present.

Major evolves through the spring and summer of 1991. The top two strips refer to the Dangerous Dogs Act that was introduced at this time.

The Haunting of the Grey Man Part One

Thatcher discovered quite soon that John Major was not as entirely in tune with her beliefs as she had thought. Thatcher was to the right on everything, from the economy through to social issues, or rather 'collection of individuals' issues (since there was no such thing as 'society'). Major had a positively pinkish tinge on many things, from race through to the need for public provision, since he had depended on it himself in his early career. With his Citizen's Charter he took to himself two of the oldest buzz words of the left and turned them into something wholly new and meaningless.

In short he was 'fiscally conservative', while being 'to the left on social issues', which is what everybody says nowadays, so he must have been ahead of his time. He may even have believed in a 'classless society', which seems perfectly reasonable to me but is anathema to vast tracts of the Conservative Party.

Burying the Bag

Major made Michael Heseltine Environment Secretary and conferred on him the task of replacing the Poll Tax. (Above, left to right: John Selwyn Gummer, Kenneth Baker, John Major, Michael Heseltine, Chris Patten, Norman Lamont and Margaret Thatcher.) These things, along with his more positive approach to Europe, really rankled with her.

Irish Myth and Legend Part Three

The Unionists were still refusing to sit down with the men of violence. They also refused to sit down with those who sit down with the men of violence.

The Selling of the Grey Man

Major and his party's poll ratings went up in the post-Gulf War absence of euphoria, and, by the autumn party conference season, Labour and the Tories were running neck and neck. The Labour Party Conference in Brighton was a peculiarly empty affair, distinguished for me by being the first time I ever sat through a speech by Tony Blair, itself peculiarly empty. I did notice his teeth for the first time. He seemed to have too many.

The selling of Major continued. At the Blackpool conference, Margaret Thatcher appeared on television for the first time since being stiffed the previous autumn. The audience went completely ape-shit, but the platform took care that she did not speak. This was High Period Major, leading up to his 'triumph' (at least that's the way it was announced on the BBC) in signing the Maastricht Treaty with various opt-outs in the area of employees' rights. He did get rid of the Poll Tax, but in every other way Majorism was just Thatcherism without Thatcher. The comic underpants obscuring the mad eyeballs.

Major came back from negotiating the Maastricht Treaty having secured opt-outs from the Social Chapter concerning employees' rights, and on European Monetary Union (EMU).

Another Election

The general election campaign of March – April 1992 was one of the
most profoundly depressing political experiences I can recall. One
would have thought it unlikely, to say the least, that a party which had
introduced the most unpopular tax in history should contrive to win
the next general election on the issue of tax, but that is what happened.

Neil Kinnock was useless, but in an entirely different way to John
Major. He just sounded useless; he didn't have that crucial track record
of uselessness in action. I always found him next to impossible to
caricature because I never had any real idea of what sort of character he
was. He started out as a lefty firebrand who delivered some memorable
sound bites ('I warn you not to be old, I warn you not to be sick' etc. in
1983 and the less successful 'I'm prepared to die for my country, but
I'm not prepared to ask my country to die for me' in 1987), but, since
his career marked a steady move away from idealistic rhetoric and
towards constrained and over-qualified bullshit, he was difficult to pin
down. After wrestling with a particularly intractable caricature of
Kinnock for several hours very late one night, I more or less gave up the
struggle and started drawing an all-purpose bald bloke with freckles.

Political Journalists

Political journalists lurk in corners whispering exclusively in one another's ears, never catching anything. They lunch frequently, drink excessively in moderation. They network from dawn to dusk, fawn contemptuously and remain supine in an upright manner until one golden day, after the spots have subsided and callow cynicism has given way to hollow realism, they acquire 'bottom'. Bottom is a certain gravitas, a certain weightiness. People with bottom become opinion formers and their views get taken into account by other people with bottom. It's circular and self-referential and at the end of the day when the world's been put to bed, made safe for government spokespersons, the difference made, they spare a thought for the constituencies and tell them about their careers.

Top left: *(left to right) Paddy Ashdown, Liberal Democrat leader, brandishing his spokesman on the economy, Alan Beith, John Major, Neil Kinnock.*

Above: *I witnessed this scene in the morning press conference on 30 March 1992 when Phil Murphy of the* Yorkshire Post *asked if the panel agreed that they'd fought a largely negative campaign. (Left to right) John Major, Chris Patten (Party Chairman), Norman Lamont (Chancellor) and Michael Heseltine.*

We Rule You, We Fool You

The actual night of the defeat was horrible, and the next day, seeing the gormless gimp Major wave at the cameras and walk back into Downing Street, was too much. *The Guardian* required an eight-column, large drawing that day, so I did one of a wedding cake, based on the old Russian anarchist drawing I remember seeing on the cover of George

Woodcock's book, *Anarchism*. I reworked the 'We Rule You, We Fool You...' idea to include honest John, with the abominable Chris Patten in a dustbin. (His defeat in Bath supplied the only light relief of the whole evening.) I've never had such a response to a drawing as I had to this one, with more requests for prints of it than for anything I've done before or since. Most of them seemed to be from people in the Labour Party.

Above: *Drawn for* The Guardian, *May 1992.*

A Pile of Pants in Our Time

Elsewhere in Europe other countries were holding referenda before ratifying the Maastricht Treaty. In Britain the recession deepened. Norman Lamont went to borrow seven billion quid off the Germans to keep the currency speculators at bay, whilst applying pressure for them to get interest rates lowered. They contemptuously shaved a quarter of one percent off the Lombard rate. The Italians were forced to devalue the lira. Major refused to take the 'soft option, the devaluers' option'…

...and was forced to drop out of the Exchange Rate Mechanism (ERM) and devalue the pound when the speculators came to call on 'Black Wednesday', 16 September 1992.

That put paid to Major's reputation as a reliable sort of chap. Suddenly the spotlight was focussed on his essential uselessness, and there it remained for the rest of his time as Prime Minister, which was an extremely long time, bearing in mind that he'd only just been re-elected. He and Lamont had cost the country billions of pounds in their failed bid to prop up the currency. They were their own tax bombshell.

Naturally Major and Lamont blamed the Germans, but the Germans didn't give a fart, so they blamed the Labour Party.

The candidates for the Labour Party leadership were (left to right): John Smith, Bryan Gould, John Prescott, Margaret Beckett and Anne Clwyd.

Newish Labour

Kinnock stood down in 1992 and John Smith was elected leader of the Labour Party. He was as unlike Kinnock as it was possible to be, as demonstrated by his body language, or rather absence of body language, during his conference speeches. Kinnock was verbose and used to wrestle with – even attempt to shag – the podium. Smith was concise, almost dour, his only sign of animation being the occasional shift of his weight from one leg to the other, rather like a small elephant in a stall. Politically there were differences. John Smith had always been an unashamed right-winger in the party, so had no need to impress the media with attacks on the left, as the former left-wing firebrand Kinnock seemed always obliged to do.

There was very little he needed to do, since the Major government started its long process of disintegration from virtually the day it was elected, needing little assistance from the opposition. Some, particularly on the right of the Labour Party, felt that this 'one more push and we're there' approach was inadequate.

John Smith was quite easy to draw. I always find it helps when a politician has glasses, since they supply a ready made frame for the rest of the caricature. This isn't the reason I was sorry when he died of a heart attack in 1994. His leadership had supplied a kind of soothing balm for the Labour Party which, after the horrors of 1992, it certainly needed. Blair, on the contrary, came equipped with a cranial drill and bucket of freezing cold water which, in my humble opinion, it certainly didn't need.

The Aftermath

Each time an election was lost meant another four or five years in which public services were going to get hammered. The Tories never said that in the manifesto of course. They intended to 'improve efficiency' and make 'vital savings' to enable them to focus spending on the 'things that really mattered'. It's a tribute to the triumph of Conservative ideology that now, twenty years on and with a Labour government finally in office, this patent balderdash is now conventional wisdom and goes largely unchallenged.

In retrospect the only redeeming aspect of the 1992 election was that, henceforth, it would be downhill all the way for honest John.

Above: At the time of Black Wednesday there was a famine going on in Somalia. This is based on a particularly haunting news image of bodies being buried there. Global foreign exchange dealings amounted to the equivalent of a trillion dollars a day.

Top right: Drawn in response to the many images of atrocity coming out of the war in Bosnia.

Bottom right: A conference on global population was held in Egypt in September 1994. This idea is lifted from a cartoon drawn by David Low in the thirties.

The Funny Looking Geezer

I'll skate over the ongoing disaster that was Majorism as briefly as possible. His principal 'achievements' during his seven years in power were rail privatisation and the Cones Hotline. I rang it once to ask what it was for, but I never got a satisfactory reply. Major was fun to draw for a while, but then it became a bit like shooting fish in a barrel. He had all sorts of awkward mannerisms and quirks of speech, and he was a funny looking geezer, but his main quality was his uselessness. He was acrobatically adept at digging holes for himself, falling down them and then struggling out again, but the humour of this spectacle palled after a while. His biggest problem was his sensitivity about his image. No, that's unfair: his biggest problem was that he was a member of the Conservative Party.

Top right: *Michael Portillo makes a show of loyalty to John Major. Drawn for* The Guardian, *May 1994*
Bottom right: *Drawn for* The Guardian, *November 1994*

The Haunting of the Grey Man Part Two

Five years is a long time to undergo slow political death. From being Honest John, the man with very few enemies who won the leadership, he became Grey Johnny No-Friends. In the Conservative Party they all hated him, even his friends, because his blundering had shown them up for what they really were. But by a cruel twist of fate he was the only man who could hold the party together, and so it went on.

Above: *(left to right) Jeffrey Archer, Nigel Lawson, Chris Patten, John Major, David Mellor, William Waldegrave, Peter Brooke, Norman Lamont, Kenneth Clarke, Douglas Hurd, Michael Heseltine, Margaret Thatcher, William Whitelaw, Virginia Bottomley, Malcolm Rifkind, Norman Fowler, Norman Tebbit, John Selwyn Gummer, Michael Howard, Nicholas Soames, Geoffrey Howe, Sir Patrick Mayhew, John Patten, Kenneth Baker, John Macgregor and Edward Heath; (at Thatcher's knee) Michael Portillo and Peter Lilley.*

Top right: *Thatcher and Tebbit were both elevated to the Lords.*

Bottom right: *The unhappy couple: Major and Lamont after Black Wednesday. Based on* The Bottle *by George Cruikshank.*

The Return of the Barmy Bovine

When Health Secretary Stephen Dorrell stood up in Parliament and announced that the most likely cause of the terrible wasting brain disease known as new variant Creutzfeldt-Jakob Disease (CJD) was the eating of dodgy beef, everybody went mad. It was such a definite statement and government statements had always been so definite that British beef was safe.

Major's first reaction was naturally to blame the Labour Party, and then, when the European Union slapped a ban on the import of British beef, he attacked Europe. The heroic wartime imagery and the subtle interplay of concerned politician and drooling cow seemed a fitting metaphor.

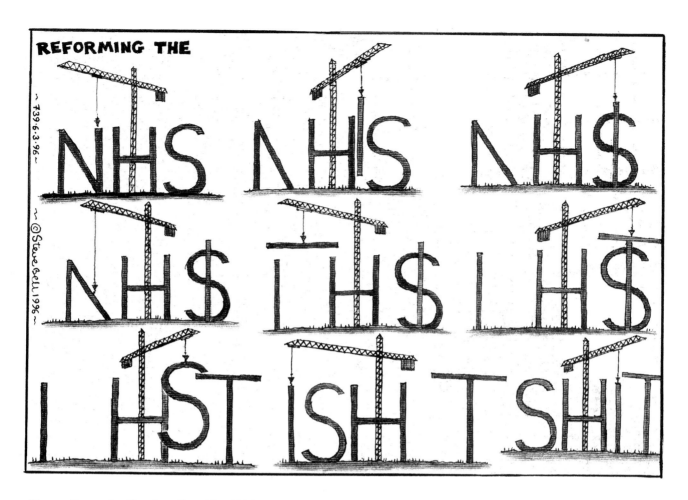

Above: *Drawn for* The Guardian, *May 1996.*

RELAUNCH FOR CONSERVATIVE MAN OF STEEL

TELEPHONE

TELEPHONE

WORLD STATESMAN SPOTTER CARD No.001

LAME DUCK PRIME MINISTER

WORLD STATESMAN SPOTTER CARD No. 002

LAME DICK PRESIDENT

892·4·2·97 ·   ~©Steve Bell 1997 ~

Major Confronts His Own End

The years wore on – Major went greyer, the Tory Party split, Major's majority slowly disappeared – until eventually it was time to face the electorate once more. This time he faced a Labour Party led by its own swivel-eyed psychopath, hungry for power and even more right-wing than he was.

Top left: *New designs for the real comic-book* Superman *were unveiled in January 1997.*

Bottom left: *Bill Clinton, US President since 1992, was having trouble with revelations about his sex life. John Major visited India and was photographed in a very stylish turban. Drawn in January 1997.*

Top: *In April 1997 I followed Paddy Ashdown on an election tour of a fish factory in Inverness.*

Middle and bottom: *There were three 'battlebuses' on the Labour campaign trail. One was called 'Leading Britain', one was called 'Into the Future' and the other was called 'With Tony Blair'.*

The election in the leafy constituency of Tatton was fought between a wide selection of loonies, including Neil Hamilton, the Tory mired in sleaze candidate, and Martin Bell, the whiter than white public virtue candidate. There were 'Vote Hamilton' posters on most of the trees in the area, but on very few human habitations. Bell won this traditionally rock-solid Tory seat by a massive margin.

Unterhosendämmerung

On Thursday 1 May 1997 the pants finally hit the shredder and burst into flames. Labour won with 418 MPs and an overall majority of 179. On the Friday morning Major went to see the Queen to hand in the keys to the kingdom, then went off to watch the cricket. The Giving Age began.

Meanwhile...
Back in the Past

The above cartoon appeared on the cover of the Christmas issue of Private Eye *in 1995. (Left to right): John Major, Michael Howard (Home Secretary), Kenneth Clarke (Chancellor), Michael Heseltine (Deputy Leader & President of the Board of Trade), Margaret Thatcher, Michael Portillo (Defence Secretary) and Virginia Bottomley (Heritage Secretary).*

The Meaning of Majorism

The Mask of Decency

Arisen without trace from Worcester Park
A bank clerk and a man who hurt his leg,
A smile to warm the cockles of your heart
With handshake strong and firm, a decent egg.
He joined the Tories, partly for a lark
And partly to rise up the greasy pole.
The party gave no succour to the poor
But nourished up this graduate of the dole
For after all, it's folk like him who vote.
He'd prove his value knocking on the door.
You cut your cloth according to your coat
And, as for deference, these days that's old hat.
Times past, we wouldn't let him sweep our moat,
Now his transparent hunger salves our fat.

Top: *Drawn for the* Guardian's Impact *magazine,*
April 1994.

Right: *Drawn for the Labour Party 1993.*

Drawn for a Guardian *Christmas special in 1994.*

This was drawn for the reborn Punch magazine in September 1996.

Left: *A combination of two cover drawings for the* New Statesman *from 1996. The cornflake box was drawn for the Labour conference issue. 'Stale old Tory craplets' was edited out for some reason.*

DON'T SEND A MONKEY TO DO THE KING OF THE JUNGLE'S JOB

During the 1997 election campaign Michael Heseltine had a brilliant idea for a poster: a photomontage of a tiny Blair sitting on the knee of a huge Helmut Kohl with the slogan 'Don't send a boy to do a man's job'.

Election 1997

The general election of 1997 was a relatively light-hearted affair. The result was never in question, and I was more than happy to witness the demise of the old enemy. I even felt a bat-squeak of sympathy for poor old John as he pluckily faced the inevitable. This time I managed to avoid the early morning press conferences and even get some day trips on battlebuses and battleplanes. I experienced the delights of a barge trip round Bristol harbour: a bargeful of hacks trailing a photogenic bargeful of the Blairs and a large group of young schoolchildren. I couldn't help but imagine the catastrophic image meltdown if the Blair barge had sunk.

I followed John Major on a visit to the Jaguar factory in Coventry, and surged round the shop floor with the media scrum that pursued him everywhere. He stopped at the place where they prepare the leather trimming, and unaccountably spent what seemed like half an hour there, fondling the material. Then he surged off and I went home. We briefly had eye contact and he had the look of a drowning man, or possibly a fish. I drew 'Feeling Boomy' on the train home.

Islington Green

Tony Blair, Tony Blair
In Islington green
Tony Blair, Tony Blair
With his hand-picked team
Loved by the Mod
Feared by the square
Tony Blair, Tony Blair
Tony Blair

Above: *Drawn for the cover of the*
New Statesman, *Christmas 1997.*
Left and Right: *Drawn for* Arts
News, *February 1997.*

Drawn for the Guardian *G2 Christmas special, 1997. Based on* The Last of England *by Ford Madox Brown and* The Scream *by Edvard Munch. (Left to right): John Prescott, Margaret Thatcher, Robin Cook, Gordon Brown, Richard Branson, Tony Blair, Geoffrey Robinson, Bernie Ecclestone, Harriet Harman, Peter Mandelson and David Blunkett.*

Above: An inquiry took place into the influence of the Freemasons in the police and judiciary. Drawn February 1998.

Below and opposite: A gallery of figures who have played their part in Northern Ireland. (Left to right): The Reverend Ian Paisley, Gerry Adams, Paddy Ashdown, who whilst an army officer on duty in the province, actually arrested John Hume and John Major. (In the styles of Marcel Duchamp, René Magritte, Damien Hirst, Jacob Epstein, Vincent Van Gogh and Sir John Lavery.) Drawn for Arts News, February 1997.

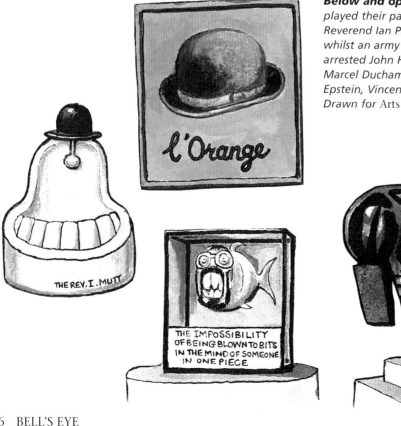

Irish Myth and Legend Part Four

The stand-off by Drumcree parish church in 1998 happened when the Orange Lodge wished to march unmolested by the forces of law and order down the nationalist Garvaghy Road, or the 'Queen's highway' as they call every road in Northern Ireland, to their local lodge in Portadown. Quite why they still believe they have this right when it no longer applies anywhere else in the UK I am at a loss to understand. The stand-off is unique in that so far the security forces have not backed down in the face of Orange pressure.

I noticed quite by accident whilst contemplating the fruit bowl that an orange rots gradually into a version of the Irish tricolour.

Lordy Hush Ma Mouth

In December 1998 William Hague took a stand on Labour's plans to reform the Lords. His objection was that the government had no plans to replace the hereditary element with anything other than more appointees, thus increasing its own patronage, and promising nothing other than a Royal Commission. The stage was set for principled guerilla action by the hereditaries, except that the Tory leader in the Lords, Lord Cranborne, had already done a deal with Labour to spare 91 hereditaries from imminent slaughter, and Hague was made to look a short, bald, incompetent chump, which was nothing new.

Above: *An idyllic July afternoon in the back garden of Number Ten Downing Street. Tony Blair calls a press conference to celebrate his achievements. After Felix Valloton.*

Below: *One of* The Owners *strips drawn for the NUJ paper the* Journalist *to commemorate Rupert Murdoch's receipt of a Papal Knighthood, as well as unwavering support from the Blair government.*

Right: *After Peter Mandelson's fall from grace, Gordon Brown was forced to sacrifice his press spokesman, Charlie Whelan, for being the original source of the story of Geoffrey Robinson's unofficial home loan to Mandelson. Drawn January 1999 in the* Guardian *and inspired by Prince Edward's engagement pictures.*

Below: *Cover of the* New Statesman, *drawn January 1999.*

Blair's Bollocks

Tony Blair described a seminal meeting during the 1992 election campaign with an 'ordinary chap polishing his Sierra' who pointed out to the Leader-to-be that the Labour Party had nothing to offer ordinary people like him who simply wanted to better themselves and their families, and said that consequently he was going to vote Conservative. It was at this moment, apparently, that Tony Blair resolved to dedicate his life to winning the confidence of people like the Sierra driver by making the Labour Party as much like the Conservative Party as possible without actually changing the name.

Right: *Drawn for 'Passing the Torch' conference, March 1997.*

Above: *Drawn for The Guardian, December 1994.*

Enter Big Ears

Blair has big ears and even bigger teeth, which is good for the purposes of caricature, but not enough. He also has something else, which I didn't spot until his first conference as Labour Party Leader at Blackpool in October 1994. It's to do with the cast of his eyes and it echoes something Thatcher has as well. Her right eye was always hooded and her left eye stared madly, at least she always did when I drew her. (I never actually saw photographic evidence until a picture by Ashley Ashwood was published in the *Financial Times* on the day she was kicked out of office. I felt triumphantly vindicated.) Tony Blair has something similar, though not as marked, and I noticed it while watching him on TV on the day of his big speech. His right eye is quite smiley and twinkly while his left eye has a more severe look. I noted this down and filed it away for future reference.

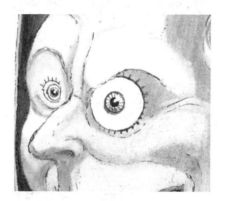

©Ashley Ashwood, *Financial Times* 1990

New Labour Pains

The 1994 conference was a watershed for Labour. In his conference speech, Blair spoke of the need to 'say what we mean and mean what we say.' What he was actually saying was revealed in briefings to selected journalists, when the announcement was made that they were going all out to amend the Labour Party constitution and get rid of the commitment to public ownership embodied in Clause Four of that document. This was to be done at a special constitutional conference to be held the following March. The atmosphere in the press room at Blackpool was fevered to say the least. Young, fresh-faced spin doctors whirled in and whirled out again, having forgotten what they were supposed to be spinning. We were spun by Jack Straw in person, who came into the *Guardian*'s cubbyhole to tell us the Party needed to 'redefine ownership'. Burglars redefine the ownership of your clock or your video when they carry it out of the window. Quite what Jack Straw meant I am still at a loss to find out.

Above, top and bottom right and top of previous page: These cartoons were all drawn at the Labour Party conference in Blackpool in 1994. The reason the tram is glowing is an attempt to render in black and white the hideous turquoise colour scheme in the conference hall.

RIGOUR, REALISM and RESPONSIBILITY.
A MEDLEY.

Believe not every Spirit, but try the Spirits whether they are of God: because many false Prophets are gone out into the World.

1 John Ch. 4 V. 1.

Design'd and Engrav'd by Wm. Hogarth.   Defaced by Steve Bell © 1997   Publish'd as the Act directs March ye 15th 1762.

Above: Drawn at the time of the special conference, held in the Methodist Central Hall in Westminster in March 1995, where the old Clause Four of the constitution, which committed the party to the principal of common ownership, was replaced with the above formulation (the right way round).

Left: Drawn (on top of Credulity, Superstition & Fanaticism *by William Hogarth) for* The Cartoonist's Progress, *an exhibition by contemporary cartoonists in tribute to Hogarth, in early 1997. Pictured are (left to right): Jack Straw, Arthur Scargill, Harriet Harman, Clare Short, Robin Cook, Ken Livingstone, Gordon Brown, Roy Hattersley, David Blunkett, Tony Blair, Margaret Beckett, Peter Mandelson and John Prescott.

Blair's Bollocks   167

The Inheritance

In practical terms New Labour meant this: it would still speak out against the privatisation of British Rail, but would give no commitment to bring it back into public ownership. This was effectively to endorse the privatisation, since no one in their right mind would have bought shares in something they knew was to return to public ownership after a change of government.

A change of government was no longer a pipe dream. Since September 1992 the Tories had been running a steady twenty-odd points behind in the polls. What it means now, is that the Blair government is as committed to privatisation as an article of faith as the Major government was. Thus, since there is very little left to privatise, the sell-offs become more and more preposterous; witness the proposed sale of the air-traffic control network and the Tote. This is the point at which I personally give up on the Labour Party.

Below: *Drawn for The Guardian, January 1996. (Left to right): Gordon Brown, Jack Straw, John Prescott, Tony Blair, Robin Cook, Harriet Harman.*

The Landslide

In the general election of 1 May 1997 Labour was triumphant. They had so many MPs that there was no room big enough to hold them all in the Palace of Westminster, so they all met up in Church House over the road, in the chamber where the Church of England Synod meets. The chamber is round and the seating is laid out in concentric circles, radiating from the podium at the centre. This had the effect of emphasising Blair's near apotheosis. Here he delivered his keynote speech: 'We were elected as New Labour and we shall govern as New Labour.' This is complete bollocks of course, as I don't recall seeing the word 'New' on the ballot paper when I voted. I viewed the proceedings from the gallery with my fellow hacks. It was very like looking down into a tin of eager, shiny baked beans.

People kept asking me if I regretted the passing of the Tories, since this seemed to mark the end of my ostensible *raison d'être* as a political cartoonist. I'm much more sympathetic to the Labour Party, I understand it, particularly since I was in it for about fifteen years; I have no sympathy at all with New Labour. That deserves the full wrath of the righteous cartoonist.

Dome Head Takes Charge

The coming of William Hague has done nothing for Tory fortunes. In cartoon terms he's a gift. His huge dome-like head, in combination with his short stature and extreme youth, make him an easy target. He isn't helped by his cast-iron self-confidence and his unfamiliarity with the concept of self-doubt, which makes you want to rub his face in something.

Above: *Based on* The Light of the World *by William Holman Hunt. Cartoonist Dave Brown first pointed out the resemblance of Hague's head to a lightbulb.*

Top left: *Hague receives the endorsement of Margaret Thatcher in the leadership contest in June 1997. Michael Howard looks on.*

Social Exclusion

New Labour social policy seemed suspiciously like Old Conservative social policy, being short on material benefits and long on exhortation. Harriet Harman, the Minister for Social Security pushed through the policies, including the withdrawal of certain benefits from single mothers – rather too vigorously for her own good – and was later dismissed for being unpopular.

Above: *Postcard design for an Economic & Social Research Council symposium on the theme of social inclusion, drawn in 1998.*

Top right: *Drawn for* The Guardian, *December, 1997.*

Bottom right: *Second from left Geoffrey Robinson, millionaire, owner of the* New Statesman, *Minister at the Department of Trade & Industry – until the news of his £370,000 home loan to Peter Mandelson broke at the end of 1998, leading to their mutual downfall.*

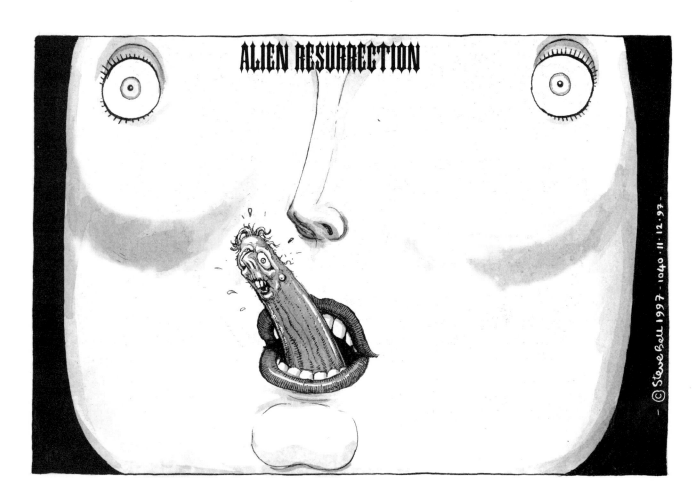

ALIEN RESURRECTION

Early Setbacks

The Formula One tobacco sponsorship fiasco smacked of the worst sort of influence-peddling when Formula One was exempted from the ban on tobacco advertising and it was revealed that Bernie Ecclestone had made a one million pound donation to the Labour Party. The Party promptly paid him his one million pounds back, which meant that he bought his influence and got his money back as well.

The first rally of the Countryside Alliance in July 1997 led to the rapid evaporation of any government support for an anti-hunting-with-hounds bill, something the Labour Party had been pledged to do since time immemorial. This hideous aggregation of fatheads, fuckwits and green-wellied, Barbour-clad buffoons who deserve nothing short of mass expropriation is just the sort Tony Blair wants on side.

Top right: The first Countryside Alliance Rally in July 1997.

Bottom right: The second Countryside Alliance rally on 1 March 1998.

The People's Death

The death of Princess Diana emphasised Blair's effortless ability to ride a wave of popularity. His air of calculated informality and, on the morning of her death, his damp-eyed 'People's Princess' sound bite contrasted favourably with the stiff-arsed approach taken by the House of Windsor. The whole country, egged on by the fourth estate, appeared to take collective leave of its senses that week. People seemed in genuine distress. But then I suppose that psycho-somatic pain is just as painful as real pain. It just isn't real, that's all.

On the Friday before the funeral I was, unusually, in the *Guardian* office, working on an eight-column special to go in the latest sixteen-page Diana pull-out section. This included the guide to where to go to ensure the best chance of being crushed to death by the six million plus people who were poised to descend on the capital (five million of them unaccountably failed to show up). Then, just on deadline time, the news came in that Mother Theresa had pegged it. Tired, cynical hacks started whooping and gibbering.

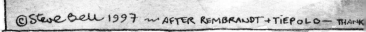

Irish Myth and Legend Part Five

The peace process made slow but definite progress through the Major years, though there was always a limit, and this was the hold the Unionists had over him in Parliament, which hold increased as his majority shrank. The ceasefire came in 1994 and went in 1996. Then it was effectively stalled until there was a change of government in the UK.

Blair and the new Northern Ireland Secretary, Mo Mowlam, were able to encourage a renewal of the IRA ceasefire and, at Easter 1998, to get all parties, including Unionists and Sinn Fein, to sign up to the Good Friday Agreement. A referendum was held and the agreement was positively endorsed by 70% of the Northern Ireland electorate.

Top left: *Mo Mowlam faces down Unionist bluster. One of the most refreshing things about Mo Mowlam is that she actually told the Reverend Ian Paisley to 'fuck off'.*
Bottom left: *In January 1998, during one particularly nasty spell of violence after the assassination in prison of the loyalist terrorist leader Billy Wright, Mo Mowlam went into the Maze to talk with loyalist paramilitary leaders.*
Above: *(left to right): David Trimble (Official Unionist leader, who apparently never wears a bowler hat), Tony Blair, Gerry Adams (Sinn Fein leader)*

Rebranding Britain

Take a bottle of loose stools laced with toenails and cold sick. Make it your life's work to denounce it publicly. Call for it to be made illegal, then take over the factory. Talk about introducing a new range of people-friendly, fibre-rich ambrosia. Invest in a new labelling machine.

Top right: *The design for the Millennium Dome was first revealed to the world at the end of October 1996.*

Bottom right: *The proposed contents of the Dome were first unveiled in February 1998. Michael Heseltine had been a long-time supporter of the Dome. Peter Mandelson was, until his fall from grace, the Minister with special responsibility for the project.*

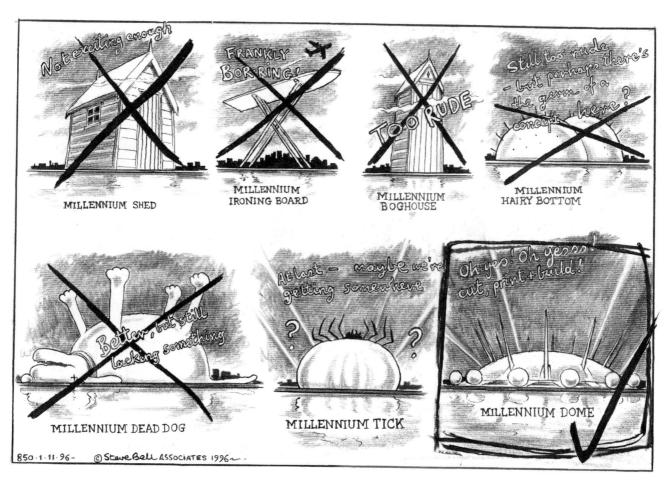

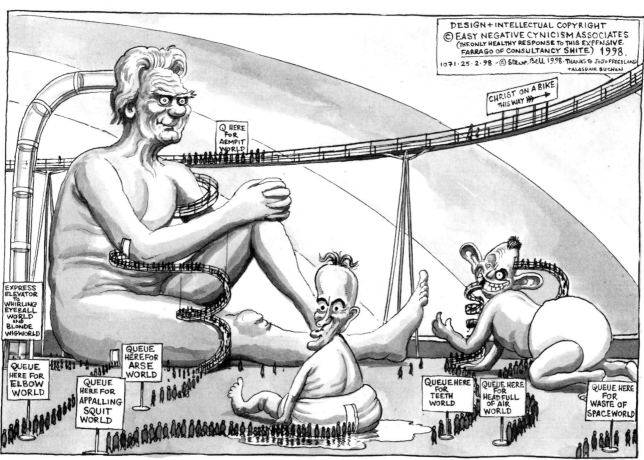

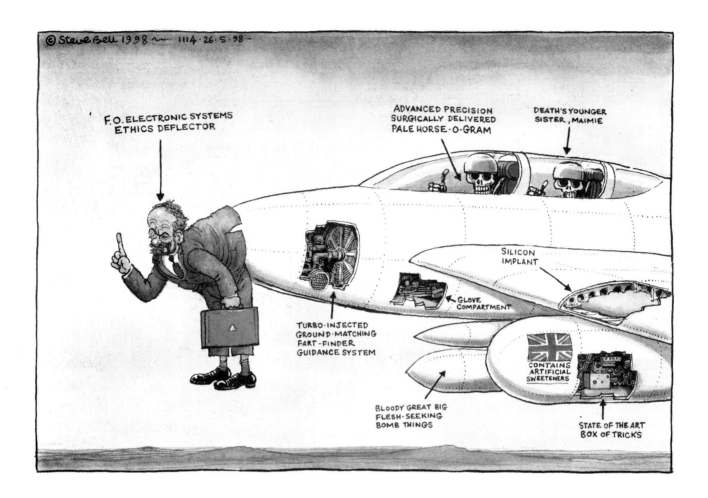

© Steve Bell 1998 ~ 1114 · 26 · 5 · 98 ~

F.O. ELECTRONIC SYSTEMS
ETHICS DEFLECTOR

ADVANCED PRECISION
SURGICALLY DELIVERED
PALE HORSE · O · GRAM

DEATH'S YOUNGER
SISTER, MAIMIE

SILICON
IMPLANT

TURBO · INJECTED
GROUND · MATCHING
FART · FINDER
GUIDANCE SYSTEM

GLOVE
COMPARTMENT

CONTAINS
ARTIFICIAL
SWEETENERS

BLOODY GREAT BIG
FLESH · SEEKING
BOMB THINGS

STATE OF THE ART
BOX OF TRICKS

Ethically Challenged

Robin Cook, left-wing fire-brand, intellectual powerhouse and connoisseur of horseflesh, became Foreign Secretary in May 1997. At a special PR launch at the Foreign Office, he announced the government's commitment to an 'ethical foreign policy'. To date this seems to consist of an enhanced commitment to the marketing of military hardware to dodgy regimes and an even more slavish attitude to US global posturing.

Bottom right: *Harriet Harman lost her job in Blair's first major reshuffle in April 1998. Based on the painting (and HMV trademark) by Francis Barraud.*

...NEITHER **LEFT**...

...NOR **RIGHT**....

...THERE IS A **THIRD WAY**.

Brown Horizons

When the weather is foul to middling and the days are short, look out to sea only to find it lost in mist. When you were young with high ideals, fired with justice and clear vision, you sensed your vocation and went into politics.

A panorama opened out for you, stretching from green to gold and blue. You sensed the heights and set to work. Now the summit approaches and all the crags are brown, not just those close to. It's a trick of the light, or is it a trick of the left?

Were you once a red? Does your residual pinkness make all you see brown?

Prudence, purpose, a package of measures, protecting the value of the people's money to provide money for what we value. Life is brown.

Or are you another lost clot in an anorak, compass broken, map upside down, chewing on your last prune, stumbling through the fog?

Bottom right: In September 1997 a particularly nasty train crash happened at Southall on the Great Western main line. The locomotive possessed safety features that would have prevented the accident, but they weren't connected up.

Statement by the Artist Formerly Known as Queen

©Steve Bell 1998 ~ 1199 · 25 · 11 · 98

The Opposition Digs in

The first lesson William Hague seems to have learnt in opposition is to enter only into alliances with those who are less popular than he is. This explains his relationship with the likes of Michael Howard, Margaret Thatcher, and, least successfully of all, with the hereditary element in the House of Lords. The other lesson he has learned from John Major is that if you're in a hole you should always smack yourself with a shovel.

Above: *Margaret Thatcher comes out in support of her old friend General Pinochet, former dictator of Chile awaiting extradition from the UK to Spain on charges of crimes against humanity.*

Bottom left: *This was drawn from life, or as near life as you can get in the House of Lords, at the State Opening of Parliament in November 1998.*

Lame Dick President

1998 was an eventful year for President William Jefferson Clinton, characterised by the almost mystical connection between revelations concerning the activities of his unruly member and renewed bombing attacks on Baghdad.

One of the least tasteful of these attacks was the one that was launched on Remembrance Day, 11 November 1998. The above drawing was prompted by television coverage of poppies cascading down in silence from the Menin Gate at Ypres on that day.

Bottom left & right: *The story of Socks, the Most Powerful Cat On Earth appears now and again over the years in the* If... *strip.*

True Bollocks

The true bollocks of Blairism lies in the fact that, while wishing to appear to be addressing the problems of poverty, inequality and lousy public service provision, it's doing the precise opposite and addressing the problems of capital. The main problem of capital is labour. This is why image is peculiarly important to New Labour, and this is exactly where political cartooning can come into its own.

And so it goes on. A year or more further on and the Labour Party are still riding high, if not even higher in the polls. Harriet Harman's gone, which is a shame, since she was good to draw (draw a square, place an eyeball in the top two corners...), Mandelson's gone, but clearly won't be gone long, so central is he to 'The Project'. The Millennium Dome is built, but still constitutes as much of a void as ever, and the government, in the person of Stephen Byers, has pronounced that it is much more interested in helping the 'wealth creators' rather than in any policy of redistribution of wealth. Thatcher's triumph is complete, her legacy safe in the hands of, paradoxically, a Labour government.

No Brains

Blair's brain in a food mixer was drawn as a cover for the *New Statesman* but it was pulled and put on an inside page. I immediately knew that the writing was on the wall for me and the *Soaraway Stoadsperson*. Apparently their marketing advice was that covers should be 'happy' with 'bright colours' and with 'not too many politicians'. In short they wanted politics with a small 'p'.

This is Blair's Bollocks with a big 'B'. Politics is about ideas and ideals. Would anybody dream of asking for ideas with a small 'i'? The thing I've always liked best about cartoons is that you can conduct arguments through them. Pictures are no different from words because they can convey all sorts of meanings, both intentional and unintentional, and can be manipulated endlessly. Images are powerful and should not be sacred. Wrestling with them inevitably flies in the face of good taste and received wisdom. Monsieur L'Artiste is an iconoclast as well as a consummate bullshitter.

It's a dirty job but somebody's got to do it. If everybody agreed with everyone about everything and offensive imagery were firmly under control it would be a sure sign that we were all dead from the neck up.

By the same author

Maggie's Farm
Further Down on Maggie's Farm
Maggie's Farm - The Last Roundup
The If… Chronicles
If… Only Again
Another Load of If…
The Unrepeatable If…
If… Bounces Back
If… Breezes In
The Vengeance of If…
The Revolutionary If…
If… Kicks Butt
If… Goes Down the John
If… Bottoms Out
For Whom Bell Tolls
The Big If…
The If… Files

With Brian Homer
Waiting for the Upturn

With Roger Woddis
Funny Old World

With Simon Hoggart
Live Briefs